ORTHO® ALL ABOUT

Perennials

Meredith® Books
Des Moines, Iowa

All About Perennials

Editor: Denny Schrock
Contributing Technical Editor: Michael D. Smith
Copy Chief: Terri Frederickson
Publishing Operations Manager: Karen Schirm
Senior Editor, Asset and Information Manager: Phillip Morgan
Edit and Design Production Coordinator: Mary Lee Gavin
Editorial and Design Assistant: Kathleen Stevens
Book Production Managers: Pam Kvitne, Marjorie J. Schenkelberg, Rick von Holdt, Mark Weaver
Contributing Copy Editor: Kelly Roberson
Contributing Technical Proofreader: Mary Meyer
Contributing Proofreaders: Fran Gardner, Ginny Perrin, Barb Rothfus
Contributing Illustrator: Jana Fothergill
Contributing Indexer: Ellen Sherron
Contributing Photo Researcher: Susan Ferguson
Contributing Photographer: Dean Schoeppner
Other Contributors: Darwin Plants, DeVroomen Plants, Kate Carter Frederick

Additional Editorial and Design Contributions from Art Rep Services
Director: Chip Nadeau
Designer: LK Design

Additional Editorial Contributions from Bittersweet Lane Publishing
Publishing Director: Michael MacCaskey
Editor: Lynn Ocone
Technical Consultant: Stephanie Cohen

Meredith® Books
Executive Director, Editorial: Gregory H. Kayko
Executive Director, Design: Matt Strelecki
Managing Editor: Amy Tincher-Durik
Executive Editor: Benjamin W. Allen
Senior Editor/Group Manager: Michael McKinley
Senior Associate Design Director: Tom Wegner
Marketing Product Manager: Brent Wiersma

Publisher and Editor in Chief: James D. Blume
Editorial Director: Linda Raglan Cunningham
Executive Director, New Business Development: Todd M. Davis
Executive Director, Sales: Ken Zagor
Director, Operations: George A. Susral
Director, Production: Douglas M. Johnston
Director, Marketing: Amy Nichols
Business Director: Jim Leonard

Vice President and General Manager: Douglas J. Guendel

Meredith Publishing Group
President: Jack Griffin
Senior Vice President: Karla Jeffries

Meredith Corporation
Chairman of the Board: William T. Kerr
President and Chief Executive Officer: Stephen M. Lacy

In Memoriam: E. T. Meredith III (1933–2003)

Note to the Readers: Due to differing conditions, tools, and individual skills, Meredith Corporation assumes no responsibility for any damages, injuries suffered, or losses incurred as a result of following the information published in this book. Before beginning any project, review the instructions carefully, and if any doubts or questions remain, consult local experts or authorities. Because codes and regulations vary greatly, you always should check with authorities to ensure that your project complies with all applicable local codes and regulations. Always read and observe all of the safety precautions provided by manufacturers of any tools, equipment, or supplies, and follow all accepted safety procedures.

Photographers

Photographers credited may retain copyright © to the listed photographs. L=Left, R=Right, C=Center, B=Bottom, T=Top

David Cavagnaro: 4-5, 19BR, 24B, 25C, 50TL, 58L, 61R, 65C, 67R, 74R, 79L, 84L, 87BR, 91C, 93C, 94L, 94R, 96R, 97L, 98L, 101R, 105R, 107C, 108L, 114L, 118C
Alan & Linda Detrick: 10T, 14-15, 20T, 50BR, 52-53, 75C, 80L, 82R, 83R, 94C, 108C, 114R
Derek Fell: 10BR, 20BL, 21BL, 21T, 62C, 66R, 85B, 91T, 104L, 114C, 117L
John Glover/Positive Images: 16T, 23B, 40, 66C, 92T, 106L, 109B, 115R
Harry Haralambou/Positive Images: 24C
Margaret Hensel/Positive Images: 25T
Jerry Howard/Positive Images: 51BR
Bill Johnson: 50BL, 77C, 81C, 86R, 92BL, 93R, 95C, 104R, 108R, 116R, 121C
Rosemary Kautzky: 6T, 17, 18TL, 22B, 28T, 41T, 61C, 62L, 69L, 75R, 77R, 83L, 84B, 86B, 100C, 100R, 105C, 111R, 115L, 117C, 117R, 120L
Bill Leaman/Positive Images: 10BL
Mike MacCaskey: 78B, 90B, 109L, 109R
Ben Philips/Positive Images: 24T
Rich Pomerantz: 11B, 11C, 11T, 18TR, 113C, 121L
Pam Spaulding/Positive Images: 50TR, 57L, 87BC
Albert Squillace/Positive Images: 90R, 102C
Peter Symcox/Positive Images: 16B
Mary Walters/Image Botanica: 59L, 64C, 75L, 77L, 80R, 88B, 92BR, 110C, 110L, 116L

All of us at Meredith® Books are dedicated to providing you with the information and ideas you need to enhance your home and garden. We welcome your comments and suggestions about this book. Write to us at:
Meredith Corporation
Meredith Gardening Books
1716 Locust St.
Des Moines, IA 50309-3023

If you would like more information on other Ortho products, call 800/225-2883 or visit us at: www.ortho.com

CONTENTS

PERENNIALS FOR ALL SEASONS

In a garden with a prominent use of perennial plants, flowers come back year after year. But that's not all perennials have to offer. Once you experiment with these plants, you'll discover how versatile they are and how they enrich your garden with more than just beautiful blooms.

For starters, you'll have the pleasure of pursuing your gardening hobby through more than one season. Months before the bright flowers of annuals such as marigolds and impatiens start to color yards, Lenten rose and catmint put on a show in the perennial garden. Long after annuals fade in late summer heat, perennial aster, sedum, and hybrid anemone make their debut. The coral bells you select for sprays of red flowers in summer will end up pleasing you with their durable winter foliage. You can also extend your gardening season by using the natural arrangements of seedpods and dried foliage that fill a perennial bed in winter as focal points.

Perennials can be a gift you pass on to another generation. Natural lifespans of perennials vary. Most live at least three years, and others are very long-lived. Some, such as peonies, can anchor a garden for decades. Just think, the lush Chinese peony that captures your imagination in spring can live for generations and become a family heirloom.

Planting a perennial is not as intimidating as planting trees or shrubs, which are much larger and have more physical impact on a garden or yard. Think of trees and shrubs in a garden like the walls and roof in a home; perennials resemble the furnishings, long-lasting but easy to change.

Increasingly, gardeners are moving perennials out of traditional beds and into larger landscape roles as foundation plants and groundcovers. Instead of pruning shrubs to keep them lower than a window ledge or narrow enough to line the sidewalk, homeowners are using perennials such as Russian sage or astilbe that provide as much interest and greenery but with more color and without the size. You may discover in your own garden that perennials such as geranium or lady's mantle are plants that can cover ground and suppress weeds while putting on a floral display. If your landscape requires a fast-growing hedge, consider ornamental grasses, which mature quickly and are easier to maintain than shrubs.

Remember the personal pleasure of gardening with perennials. You can make your garden a haven of learning for the family. Your plants will attract wildlife, such as songbirds drawn to black-eyed susan seeds or butterflies to joe-pye weed blossoms. Learn plant lore to tell your children, such as the tales linked to bleeding heart and the ancient myths surrounding plants such as peony, mountain bluet, and yarrow.

Ultimately, perennial gardening is a rewarding hobby that transforms your yard into a setting where fun, satisfaction, and beauty prevail.

This book will help you reap the most from your efforts by showing how to plant, select, and care for perennials suited to your site and budget. Here's your chance to learn time-honored and cutting-edge techniques that will make your perennial garden a showplace!

▼ **By late summer, the green-and-white leaves of miscanthus surge skyward in front of black-eyed susan, joe-pye weed, and Russian sage.**

SPRING, FIRST FLOWERS

In early spring, garden beds and borders green up fast. Spring flowers are not limited to trees and shrubs or bulbs. Sleepy perennials stretch skyward as temperatures rise. Some, the hardiest, begin to bloom as the snow melts. Others leaf out quickly, their fresh foliage followed by plump buds and cheerful flowers.

Look to nature and you'll find plenty of perennial early risers, such as trillium and marsh marigold. Dozens of other native species flower in spring, as do their hybrid cousins.

To learn which early bloomers are suited to your region and climate, spend some time at a local nursery or botanical garden. Mail-order and online catalogs will increase choices, as will plant swaps. If you live in a mild climate, there will be a plentiful variety to choose from. Regardless of where you reside, the hunt for perennials that bloom early is itself a reward.

▲ Blue star contrasts with the bright yellows and golds of early spring daisies.

◀ Pastel primroses make a multicolored carpet beneath a flowering cherry tree.

Combine early bloomers for impact

To develop vivid, early color, arrange first-flowering plants in clusters; plant those with similar needs and compatible colors together. Group all plants in sufficient quantities to make an impact instead of scattering sparse patches in the garden.

■ **Take a cue from nature.** Your garden plantings can be sandwiched into the same piece of ground. First flowers are followed by second and third waves of other plants in the same location. Consider tucking clumps of early-blooming perennials between larger, later-rising plants; even as flowers fade, the foliage remains as a groundcover.

Blue star retains its willowlike foliage long after its clusters of blue flowers fade. And, after the spring blooms of columbine fade, the leaves continue to provide interest throughout the summer.

EARLY BLOOMERS

Blue star *(Amsonia)*	Bleeding heart *(Dicentra)*
Hybrid columbine *(Aquilegia)*	Leopard's bane *(Doronicum)*
Wall rock cress *(Arabis)*	Lenten rose *(Helleborus)*
Basket-of-gold *(Aurinia)*	Moss phlox *(Phlox)*
False indigo *(Baptisia)*	Primrose *(Primula)*
Brunnera *(Brunnera)*	Lungwort *(Pulmonaria)*
Marsh marigold *(Caltha)*	Trillium *(Trillium)*
Lily-of-the-valley *(Convallaria)*	Globeflower *(Trollius)*

EARLY SUMMER COLOR

By early summer, many gardens burst with roses, lilies, and honeysuckle, but perennials, too, contribute fragrance and vibrant color. In addition to the much-loved Chinese peonies, foxgloves, and coral bells, you'll find lesser-grown gems on the list below.

Some gardeners select flowers that bloom at approximately the same time for a garden filled with color. This creates a spectacular, but brief, display. Unfortunately, it also means little or no perennial bloom for the rest of the season. Gardeners who prefer a longer duration of early summer color plant for a continuous succession of bloom, with new flowers coming as spring flowers fade.

While this may seem to dilute the impact of the overall color scheme, it actually reveals more of the character of the plants.

In general, even when the garden is planned and planted with bloom succession in mind, there may still be three or four peak periods of flowering during the season, interspersed with spans of quiet green relief.

Sequencers—plants that contribute to the scheme throughout the seasons—help bridge the gap between these peak periods.

▲ Chartreuse plumes of lady's mantle sprawl, contrasting in both color and shape with vertical spikes of foxglove.

▶ Showy orange cups of Oriental poppy combine with purple and lavender iris and lilac spikes of gas plant in this early summer garden.

◀ Lucious, full, fragrant flowers of Chinese peony are produced by hardy and long-lived plants with sturdy green foliage.

As a guideline, perennials with enduring and interesting foliage, such as ferns, ornamental grasses, lady's mantle, lamb's-ears, and meadow rue, are excellent sequencers. Meadow rue, for example, provides an airy scrim that adds a sense of mystery to a small garden and screens sweeps of browning bulb foliage.

Make it last

With a little help, many perennials that flower in early summer will continue or repeat flowering over a long season. Consider the hybrid 'Rozanne' geranium that bears clusters of bright violet-purple flowers starting in early summer. In cool-summer regions it will continue flowering for weeks. And, if cut back once the flowering lags, the plant will regrow and bloom again later.

Catmint (*Nepeta* 'Blue Wonder') is a good multiseason plant. It starts blooming in spring like many other perennials. But if spent flowers are removed it will bloom again in fall, sometimes just as heavily as it did in spring. Cut spent stems in half to keep blooms coming.

EARLY SUMMER BLOOMERS

Lady's mantle (*Alchemilla*)	Coral bells (*Heuchera*)
Goatsbeard (*Aruncus*)	Inula (*Inula*)
Astilbe (*Astilbe*)	Crested iris (*Iris*)
Bellflower (*Campanula*)	Japanese water iris (*Iris*)
Threadleaf coreopsis (*Coreopsis*)	Siberian iris (*Iris*)
Delphinium (*Delphinium*)	Common sundrops (*Oenothera*)
Pinks (*Dianthus*)	Chinese peony (*Paeonia*)
Strawberry foxglove (*Digitalis*)	Oriental poppy (*Papaver*)
Dropwort (*Filipendula*)	Common beard tongue (*Penstemon*)
Geranium (*Geranium*)	

HIGH-SUMMER DISPLAY

High summer is showtime in the garden: To create that dazzling array of nonstop fireworks, pay attention to the average bloom times of your favorite perennials. Once you know how they behave in your own backyard, you can devise powerful combinations, interweaving flowers and foliage. When one plant finishes blooming, another can step in and take its place. Track performance in a garden journal or notebook and use the Bloom Season Chart on pages 12 and 13 to help plan your display.

Plant a variety of performers

The best way to enjoy an unbroken sequence of bloom is to develop a full palette of perennial color. Variety helps ensure that despite quirky weather, disease, or nuisance animals, something will succeed. Begin with plants that have staying power. Yarrow, sedum, daylily, and

▲ **Every garden is at its showy best at least once a year, usually summer. Here, shasta daisy, yellow loosestrife, and rose campion mix with annuals and groundcovers.**

▶ **Some varieties of daylily begin blooming in early summer and continue to bloom well into fall.**

◀ **A grouping of pink astilbe brightens a shaded border.**

similar tireless plants come in a range of sizes and colors.

■ **Don't stop with color.** Group your choices by shape and texture as well. Many perennials are basically mound-shape and need contrast to keep their own identity. Choose ostrich fern, sea holly, and perennial fountain grass for a textural change of pace.

Sun or shade?

Sunny gardens can host a tremendous number of summer bloomers. Among them are many native flowers that grow larger and bloom longer than they do in the wild. Purple coneflower, blanket flower, black-eyed susan, and common beard tongue all provide multiple possibilities throughout the summer season.

Shady woodland gardens are often quite dry by midsummer. Where water is an issue, select drought-tolerant plants such as barrenwort or yellow archangel. If you have damp shade, dozens of perennials suit it, from spiky ligularia to bold rodgersia. Damp or dry, shade gardens can hold marvelous tapestries of foliage perennials such as hosta and lungwort. For contrast, mix in rounded and ruffled coral bells and fine-textured astilbe.

Late Summer

▶ Rich reds and golds of chrysanthemums, or just plain "mums," are a fall classic in the perennial garden.

◀ White plumes of miscanthus flowers catch every breeze, while joe-pye weed and fleeceflower contribute reds and magentas to the fall garden scene.

A s late summer melts into autumn, warm days and cool nights waken the hidden flames of foliage. Blue star and balloon flower turn golden and the leaves of Japanese blood grass are at their finest red. But perennial flowers bloom too.

To have a good show in autumn, you must dedicate significant garden space to some of these late bloomers. It need not mean a summer sacrifice: If 10 to 20 percent of your plants offer strong fall flower or foliage color, they will carry the season. Keep in mind, many late performers are large plants with plenty of character. They are standouts. What's more, you can place them behind rebloomers, such as yarrow, blanket flower, and daylily, whose contribution will now be amplified by their dramatic neighbors.

▼ Colorful fall flowers of sedums, joe-pye weed and white spires of Kamchatka bugbane mingle with and contrast with ornamental grasses.

To maximize your autumn display, group late bloomers in clusters and sweeps, and give them supportive companions (such as long-season foliage plants and additional reliable rebloomers), so the fall performers do not appear as an afterthought in the home landscape. Select fall flowers that can pull their weight over several seasons, such as sedum and black-eyed susan.

Autumn stars

Native plants excel in the autumn landscape. The golden tassels of goldenrod burn against the sky, and asters haze the garden with smoky blue and purple. Varieties of native switch grasses, such as 'Heavy Metal' and 'Northwind', shimmer like spun gold. Indeed, a host of other grasses bring glitter and gleam to fall gardens, from miscanthus such as 'Morning Light' or 'Silberfeder' to dwarfs such as Mexican feather grass.

In shady gardens, bugbane and the white flowers of fragrant hosta scent the air. With rosy or creamy flowers, hybrid anemone blooms long and hard in dappled light. Arching wands of Japanese toad lily are studded with tiny flowers. And when the foliage tapestry is turning golden, there are evergreen ferns and Lenten roses to carry on the spectacle through winter.

LATE-BLOOMING PERENNIALS

Monkshood *(Aconitum)*
Kamchatka bugbane *(Actaea)*
Hybrid anemone *(Anemone)*
New England aster *(Aster)*
Boltonia *(Boltonia)*
Leadwort *(Ceratostigma)*
Helenium *(Helenium)*
Cardinal flower *(Lobelia)*
'Autumn Fire' Sedum *(Sedum)*
Goldenrod *(Solidago)*
Japanese toad lily *(Tricyrtis)*

WINTER INTEREST

Winter is an excellent time to study the flow and follow-through of garden color. Journal notes will help you rule out less suitable varieties and rearrange better performers for winter appeal. Through selection and editing, you can develop your own winter perennial palette to enliven this underappreciated season. By leaving seedheads in place, you'll experience the life and moving color of birds visiting the winter garden.

As you expand your palette with off-season performers, you may need to make room by cutting back on spring- and summer-blooming flowers. Start by replacing plants that no longer thrill you, supplanting them with late bloomers. Take advantage of winter's downtime to study specialty catalogs for plants to try. Before long, the flow of overlapping color will extend throughout the seasons.

Winter in the garden does not need to be a barren time. The winter garden's subtle beauty lies in line and form. Cold-winter gardens can hold eye-catching shapes and textures, especially from grasses such as maidengrass and feather reed grass. When sturdy, structural perennials are left to stand through wind, snow, and ice, the resulting shapes can work magic, transforming a meadow from stubble to sculpture.

Woodland winters are wonderfully quiet. Grasses whisper in the breeze, their hollow stems rustling softly. Blanketing snow emphasizes the graceful silhouette of purple coneflower, with its stems the color of burnt earth. Brown and burnished, the skeletons of joe-pye weed cast shadows on the snow, joined by native goldenrod.

Where mild winters are the rule (Zones 7, 8, and 9), the garden possibilities become far more plentiful. Evergreen perennials come into their own when earlier-blooming, brasher competition retreats. Grouped and given the support of compact border shrubs (evergreen herbs, rhododendrons, and dwarf conifers), even the least showy winter flowers can make a cheerful splash.

▲ **Consider the merits of a garden covered with snow. Such a display is a reality for northern-tier gardeners, and a source of special beauty.**

▶ **Lenten rose or hellebore is a welcome harbinger of spring. Its late-winter flowers are often caught— and dusted—by late-season snow.**

◀ **Faded, dried flowers of many perennials are beautiful in their own right. Beyond that, the seeds they contain are an important food source for many species of birds.**

FINE-TUNING MULTISEASON APPEAL

If color themes are to change with the seasons, timing becomes critical. The chart on pages 12 and 13 is a good way to begin your color plan. It ranks the perennials in this book in order of their bloom, from early spring through late fall.

For a real-world guide to bloom sequence take your cues from nature. Observe the natural areas that are near where you live. In the woodlands, prairies, mountains, or chaparral nearby, watch and you'll see the season unfold in a way that is likely to be directly applicable to your own garden.

Also notice how in nature perennials grow with grasses, annuals, bulbs, and shrubs. A successful perennial garden mimics nature's patterns and its most attractive vignettes, but edits out the unattractive gaps.

What happens in your garden is specific to your region and climate. The best way to track performance is by keeping regular records in a garden journal. You don't need to make voluminous notes, and you don't have to write in it every day; simply follow these guidelines:

▌ Record what you've planted, along with rainfall and temperature.

▌ Note what's in bloom and when so you can gradually learn the general flow of each season through the year.

▌ Take snapshots to remember where and when plants bloomed. Study them to plan new combinations.

▌ Keep a calendar in the garage or shed in order to indicate your maintenance and fertilizer schedules from year to year.

▌ Jot down the first and last blooming dates of all perennials each year. Patterns will emerge, and soon you'll be better able to combine plant selections to extend the season of interest.

▌ Mass similar flowers. Planting in drifts—grouping like flowers or planting several plants of one perennial species together—is one way to create mass. Drifts have more power than single blooms. For a natural effect, mass flowers in asymmetrical drifts flowing in and out of other flower groups. Use odd numbers of plants arranged densely in the middle and more sparsely near the edges of the bed.

▶ By fall, neat boundries between plants have long disappeared as larger plants have reached full size. Thinleaf sunflower dominates the far end, while a range of perennials, including garden phlox and aster, add to the cacophony throughout.

▲ In spring, well before the season is in full swing, the beds and formal design create a pleasing structure for the garden. The mostly green garden is punctuated with the color of Chinese peonies and bearded iris.

▲ In midsummer the yellow of daylilies plays off the royal blue of delphiniums, while astilbe fills in with rust and pale tones.

BLOOM SEASON CHART

Use this chart to help you plan overlapping seasons of bloom for color all year. Because perennials are listed in relative order of bloom, you can easily see at a glance which bloom together, which bloom in succession, and which bloom for extra-long times. Remember that any bloom chart will be only a rough guide, as bloom seasons can differ according to the region, weather, microclimates, and cultivars. Green bars represent bloom seasons; orange bars represent fall foliage and fruit effects.

Plant Name	Spr. E M L	Sum. E M L	Fall E M L	Win. E M L
Lenten rose (Helleborus orientalis)				
Great white trillium (Trillium grandiflorum)				
Basket-of-gold (Aurinia saxatilis)				
Bergenia (Bergenia)				
Marsh marigold (Caltha palustris)				
Red barrenwort (Epimedium × rubrum)				
Cushion spurge (Euphorbia polychroma)				
Wall rock cress (Arabis caucasica)				
Moss phlox (Phlox subulata)				
Lungwort (Pulmonaria saccharata)				
Brunnera (Brunnera macrophylla)				
Old-fashioned bleeding heart (Dicentra spectabilis)				
Lily-of-the-valley (Convallaria majalis)				
English primrose (Primula vulgaris)				
Hybrid columbine (Aquilegia hybrids)				
Blue false indigo (Baptisia australis)				
Crested iris (Iris cristata)				
Cheddar pink (Dianthus gratianopolitanus)				
Thrift (Armeria maritima)				
Globeflower (Trollius)				
Foam flower (Tiarella)				
Lady's mantle (Alchemilla mollis)				
Blue star (Amsonia tabernaemontana)				
Astilbe (Astilbe × arendsii)				
Great masterwort (Astrantia major)				
Yellow corydalis (Corydalis lutea)				
Japanese primrose (Primula japonica)				
Peach-leaf bellflower (Campanula persicifolia)				
Centranthus (Centranthus ruber)				
Twinspur (Diascia hybrids)				
Common foxglove (Digitalis purpurea)				

Plant Name	Spr. E M L	Sum. E M L	Fall E M L	Win. E M L
Southern lupine (Thermopsis caroliniana)				
Bloody cranesbill (Geranium sanguineum)				
'Johnson's Blue' geranium (Geranium 'Johnson's Blue')				
Geum (Geum)				
Foxtail lily (Eremurus × isabellinus)				
Coral bells (Heuchera hybrids)				
Bearded iris (Iris germanica)				
Siberian iris (Iris sibirica)				
Hybrid lupine (Lupinus Russell hybrids)				
Catmint (Nepeta × faassenii)				
Chinese peony (Paeonia lactiflora)				
Oriental poppy (Papaver orientale)				
Common beard tongue (Penstemon)				
Lamb's-ears (Stachys byzantina)				
Rodgersia (Rodgersia aesculifolia)				
Solomon's seal (Polygonatum odoratum)				
'Coronation Gold' yarrow (Achillea × 'Coronation Gold')				
Hollyhock (Alcea rosea)				
Goatsbeard (Aruncus dioicus)				
Meadow sage (Salvia nemerosa)				
Hybrid bee delphinium (Delphinium elatum)				
Butterfly weed (Asclepias tuberosa)				
English lavender (Lavandula angustifolia)				
Golden marguerite (Anthemis tinctoria)				
Mullein (Verbascum)				
Carpathian bellflower (Campanula carpatica)				
Common yarrow (Achillea millefolium)				
Maiden pink (Dianthus deltoides)				
Allwood pink (Dianthus × allwoodii)				
Baby's breath (Gypsophila paniculata)				
Shasta daisy (Leucanthemum × superbum)				
Caucasian leopard's bane (Doronicum orientale)				
Threadleaf coreopsis (Coreopsis verticillata)				

Plant Name	Spr. E M L	Sum. E M L	Fall E M L	Win. E M L	Plant Name	Spr. E M L	Sum. E M L	Fall E M L	Win. E M L
'Rozanne' hybrid geranium (Geranium × 'Rozanne')					Perennial sunflower (Helianthus × multiflorus)				
Daylily (Hemerocallis)					Thinleaf sunflower (Helianthus decapetalus)				
Japanese water iris (Iris ensata)					Wall germander (Teucrium chamaedrys)				
Knautia (Knautia macedonica)					Hardy hibiscus (Hibiscus moscheutos)				
Torch lily (Kniphofia uvaria)					Liatris (Liatris spicata)				
Common sundrops (Oenothera fruticosa)					Ligularia (Ligularia)				
Hollyhock mallow (Malva alcea)					Cardinal flower (Lobelia cardinalis)				
Yellow patrinia (Patrinia)					Purple ice plant (Delosperma cooperi)				
Pincushion flower (Scabiosa columbaria)					Switch grass (Panicum virgatum)				
Brazilian verbena (Verbena bonariensis)					Perennial fountain grass (Pennisetum alopecuroides)				
Long-leaf speedwell (Veronica longifolia)					Garden phlox (Phlox paniculata)				
Feather reed grass (Calamagrostis)					Cupid's dart (Catananche caerulea)				
Lilac sage (Salvia verticillata)					Balloon flower (Platycodon grandiflorus)				
Blanket flower (Gaillardia aristata)					Black-eyed susan (Rudbeckia fulgida)				
'Frances Williams' hosta (Hosta sieboldiana 'Frances Williams')					Silver spike grass (Spodiopogon sibiricus)				
Crocosmia (Crocosmia × crocosmiiflora)					Anise hyssop (Agastache foeniculum)				
Tufted hair grass (Deschampsia caespitosa)					Ornamental oregano (Origanum laevigatum)				
Globe thistle (Echinops ritro)					Helenium (Helenium autumnale)				
Fleabane (Erigeron hybrids)					Miscanthus (Miscanthus sinensis)				
'Autumn Fire' sedum (Sedum 'Autumn Fire')					Goldenrod (Solidago hybrids)				
Sea lavender (Limonium latifolium)					Three-veined everlasting (Anaphalis triplinervis)				
Leadwort (Ceratostigma plumbaginoides)					Fragrant hosta (Hosta plantaginea)				
Queen-of-the-prairie (Filipendula rubra)					Showy sedum (Sedum spectabile)				
Blue oat grass (Helictotrichon sempervirens)					Monkshood (Aconitum)				
Variegated purple moor grass (Molinia caerulea 'Variegata')					Aster (Aster)				
Bee balm (Monarda didyma)					Boltonia (Boltonia asteroides)				
Russian sage (Perovskia atriplicifolia)					Northern sea oats (Chasmanthium latifolium)				
Rodgersia (Rodgersia pinnata)					Hybrid anemone (Anemone × hybrida)				
Stoke's aster (Stokesia laevis)					Rose turtlehead (Chelone obliqua)				
Plume poppy (Macleaya cordata)					Meadow rue (Thalictrum rochebrunianum)				
Giant feather grass (Stipa gigantea)					Japanese toad lily (Tricyrtis hirta)				
Chinese astilbe (Astilbe chinensis)					Hardy ageratum (Eupatorium coelestinum)				
New York ironweed (Vernonia noveboracensis)					Kamchatka bugbane (Actaea simplex)				
Purple coneflower (Echinacea purpurea)					Hardy chrysanthemum (Chrysanthemum hybrids)				
Amethyst sea holly (Eryngium amethystinum)					Himalayan fleeceflower (Persicaria affinis)				
					Gulf muhly (Muhlenbergia capillaris)				

DESIGN STRATEGIES

Why and how do you want to use perennials? What short- and long-range goals will these versatile plants help you meet? To answer these questions, begin by visualizing your entire landscape.

You might already know what's there, but take the time to really see your yard. Identify the elements you plan to keep, such as trees, sidewalks, outbuildings, the swimming pool, the water garden, fences, and other components. Next, list problem areas and any areas you dislike, such as patches of bare ground, gaps between existing plants and your lawn, shady spots under trees, wet or dry pockets where nothing seems to grow, weedy or unkempt areas, or spots where the landscape seems drab.

As you examine your yard, think about what perennials offer. They are better solutions for some problems than for others, and they do more than perk up problem areas. For example, they may be the best choice for soggy or dry soil.

To get the best performance from your garden, examine all aspects of a perennial, not just its flower colors. It's the whole plant—texture, form, structure, and foliage—and its placement that completes the yard. Keep in mind that the same plant that works at the back of a bed with only a side view may also belong in the center of a bed that will be seen from all sides.

The purpose of your perennial garden and your expectations define its limits, including shape and placement on your lot. A cheerful entry garden with a nicely landscaped front path will be visible to friends and strangers alike. A garden for meditating, on the other hand, requires privacy.

Practical considerations may also dictate your garden design. To create views from indoors, determine where you like to sit or stand inside your house, and plan and plant your vistas accordingly.

No matter how perfect your garden design in your imagination or on paper, it will change season by season. Some plants will thrive, and others won't. Weather, pests, or some other unpredictable event will occur. All of these factors will affect your design.

Many gardeners focus on the design details, namely the specific plants and flowers. But by learning to see your garden on another level, as a series of shapes and patterns instead of the details, changes wrought by happenstance will be both less significant and easier to adapt to.

Perennial gardens are, above all, a dynamic project. Gardening is particpating in the show and gardens are never "done." Ongoing alterations that accommodates natural change—thinning, replacing, and adding—are the soul of gardening and the essence of a successful perennial garden.

▼ **Artfully combining flower colors, leaf shapes and textures, and plant heights is the key to successful design with perennials.**

FORMAL OR INFORMAL?

Formal gardens are architectural, extending the rooms of the house they surround. Usually a formal garden has symmetrical balance, with plantings on one side of a main axis mirroring plantings on the other side. Pruning transforms shrubs into topiaries or hedges into outlines for geometrically shaped beds and walkways.

In contrast, informal gardens rely on a more naturalistic arrangement of plants. When pruning plants in informal settings, gardeners enhance their natural forms rather than carving new shapes. Informality lends itself to curving paths and borders that flow with the terrain.

In practice, many gardens are combinations of both styles. Symmetry and geometry work well near the house, and free-flowing lines and looser edges dominate farther away.

Lines in the garden

Gardens are composed of many lines. Lines are edges that your eye naturally follows. The concept is easier to understand if you think of line as an outline. It's not quite the same thing as shape, which is three-dimensional. Instead, it's the edge of the bed and the silhouette of plants and other features in and around a garden.

Horizontal lines are parallel to the ground. They can be far above the ground,

▲ **Formal designs begin with straight-edge beds and a focal point.**

▼ **Informal designs feature curving beds and plants spilling over edges.**

such as a broad, dense tree canopy or the top of an enclosed arbor. On the ground, garden pathways are the most obvious example of horizontal lines.

Bed lines are an important type of horizontal line. These are the lines you create when shaping planting areas, formed by the separation between lawn and planting area or between paving and planting. They may be formed of stone, brick, plastic, or metal edging, or one could be a simple line cut with a shovel.

Use smooth curving lines to give the perennial garden a serene, informal look. Sweeping bed lines and meandering paths are characteristic of gardens featuring curvilinear edges.

Straight lines with sharp angles and corners suggest activity. They are contemporary and formal in feel and speed your eye through the landscape. Straight lines connected to symmetrical curves are called arc-and-tangent, and they are used in formal gardens.

Vertical lines keep a garden from becoming boring. As accents, they create a rhythm, moving the eye up and down and through the plants in the garden. The most apparent vertical lines in a landscape are vines and the trunks of trees. Posts, arbors, fences, or walls form other vertical lines. Though they run up and down, vertical lines don't have to be perfectly straight.

PLANTING IN TIERS

◄ Arrange perennials according to height, placing tall plants, such as miscanthus, at the rear, and lower plants, such as catmint at the front edge. Garden phlox and asters provide medium-size plants.

Perennials are most often grown with other kinds of plants, roughly in order of height. For simplicity's sake, these layers are called first, second, and third tiers. In either formal or naturalistic gardens, planting in tiers creates a relaxed, abundant look, as exemplified by a meadow or woodland.

The first tier serves as a carpet, where low-growing plants creep and sprawl, defining edges and lacing layers of the bed together. The middle tier of intermediate-size plants provides a ladder between the front and back tiers. This middle layer is like the forest understory, knit from compact shrubs and perennials. The third tier creates a canopy, or skyline, of the tallest plants. It often includes evergreen trees and shrubs that enclose the space like a hedge, rise to the high point in the center of an island, or form a backdrop in the border.

In a large garden, each tier can be full-size. In a smaller garden, you must scale the tiers down; use shrubs to play the role of trees, and narrow, space-saving plants to substitute for plumper ones.

The third tier

Begin with this tier, establishing the garden line and creating a powerful silhouette.

Skyline plantings integrate the garden with surrounding trees or buildings. They enclose the garden and bring it into balance within the scale of its location. Well-chosen backdrop plantings not only provide a supportive framework, but they also can take a leading role with dramatic floral displays all their own.

Big plants create a visual stop, framing a bed or border by blocking out distractions such as cars and road signs. Traditional garden design relies on shrubs and trees for the background, but many large perennials can serve the same purpose.

In large yards, tall ornamental grasses—with their bursts of color, great stature, and changing seasonal interests—are natural candidates to provide screening, privacy, and a backdrop for flowerbeds. Some late-blooming goldenrods raise their heads high, while joe-pye weed looms taller still, producing a great mist of lavender-purple flowers about 5 feet above the ground. Plume poppy, an impressive third-tier perennial, can reach 10 feet tall with large, heart-shape leaves and long plumes of cream-color flowers.

Many large perennials spend spring and summer on vegetative growth, climbing skyward, reserving their bloom for late summer or autumn. These plants offer flowers or foliage in the fall, when this framework takes the spotlight.

Whatever the style of your garden, be aware of scale. Overly large plants can smother plants in other tiers. The progression of perennials should be gradual between tiers.

In island beds of mixed plantings, the tallest plants need to be toward the center where they won't obscure shorter ones. In smaller spaces, a 4-foot wall of blue false indigo will provide a natural screen, with dark blue, pealike flowers in early summer. Airy masses of Brazilian verbena weave into a fine scrim, veiling everything that lies behind them in a shimmering haze of purple-blue clusters.

First and second tiers

First- and second-tier plants should merge with third-tier plantings, easing the eye toward the ground. Within a garden, layers create an inner topography that plays up shape and texture. Relaxed interior arrangements create a fascinating flow of form as well as color.

▲ At the path's edge, low-growing lady's mantle and variegated hakone grass are backed by hostas and, in the rear, a weeping spruce.

▲ Perennials that bloom at the same time when planted in tiers create a wall of color that the eye can absorb in a glance.

Second-tier plantings are an intermediate layer between the first tier and the back border, creating a transition between the backdrop and the edge. In larger gardens, there may be two or three intermediate levels. In smaller beds, one second tier will be plenty.

In formal plantings, make the intermediate layer uniform in height and

▲ Use the contours of your yard, natural or not, to mimic the effect of tier planting.

shape. Arrange plants in patterns that best show off the qualities that catch your eye.

Front and midborder plants often display a charming informality. Edge the front of a bed or border using low-growing plants with foliage textures and colors that contrast with the lawn or pathway. Lamb's-ears, with its silver-furred leaves, is a favorite edger. Coral bells is another exquisite choice. First-tier edging plants can form a continuous strip along the garden's front border for a formal effect; however, a combination of low-growing plants is also pleasing. Alternate clusters of different types of plants to create a subtle edge, but one that clearly states where the garden begins and ends.

MOUNDERS AND SPRAWLERS

Silver mound artemisia *(Artemesia)*
Basket-of-gold *(Aurinia)*
Carpathian bellflower *(Campanula)*
Bloody cranesbill *(Geranium)*
Baby's breath *(Gypsophila)*
Evergreen candytuft *(Iberis)*
Catmint *(Nepeta)*
Moss phlox *(Phlox)*

THE POWER OF SHAPE

As you think about overall garden design—the interplay between tiers—contrasting shapes play a major role. In fact, many savvy garden designers concentrate more on the shape of perennials than on any other feature, even color.

You can obtain the shape you want, of course, by shearing, but that's repetitive work and stresses the plants. It's far easier to start with shapes bestowed by nature instead of those imposed by human hands.

Though perennials grow in a myriad of forms, it's easy to remember some basic shapes. Plants described as architectural have a framework with definitive lines, such as upright feather reed grass. Eccentric plants, such as sea holly and purple coneflower, also have a strong framework but branch more freely.

Some plants resemble fans and fountains in their growth. The foliage of fan-shaped plants tends to be flat and upright, whereas that of fountain plants shoots out in different directions.

Turret-shape blazing star and torch lily, which are reminiscent of castle towers, produce slender spikes that add vertical interest to the garden by reaching upward. Mounders, on the other hand, stay low and rounded, like half a sphere. Sprawlers are looser and almost seem to hug the ground.

Use perennial shapes to contrast with one another. Fans and fountains, mounds and sprawlers, sturdy towers and slim turrets—all can be endlessly recombined into exciting partnerships.

Pair a fan-shape iris with foamy baby's breath. Silky Mexican feather grass softens look and line, and structural 'Autumn Fire' sedum adds strength. Large, striking plants such as 'Superba' featherleaf rodgersia require equal partners to keep them balanced. Large-scale plants with different textures and colors—for instance,

▲ **Bold spikes of delphinium rise above mounding perennials, punctuating the scene with purple exclamation points.**

feathery hay-scented fern and bold-leaved ligularia—work well together. So will large masses of smaller plants, such as cranesbill or astilbe. Eccentric flower spires of mullein become magnificent when contrasted with large and simple miscanthus.

Flower shapes and sizes also contribute to your garden's design. Plants may bear multiple or single blooms that are flat, round, clustered, bell-shape, or cuplike; tiny or large. Foliage is just as diverse.

Take advantage of the freedom to experiment. Combine plants with patience and soon you'll have a garden that is uniquely yours.

Artful use of texture

Skillfully combining textures enhances a garden's charm. Take both the flowers and the foliage into account. For perennials in particular, foliage is on view far longer than flowers. To achieve a harmonious yet eye-catching look, combine coarse plants with plants of medium or fine texture. An example is planting shade-loving brunnera with its large, heart-shape leaves, adjacent to a perennial with lacy or ferny foliage, such as astilbe or maidenhair fern.

◀ **Use contrasting shapes to add visual interest to your garden. The bold leaves of hosta are matched with the delicate tracery of astilbe.**

▶ **Wiry, vertical stems of feather reed grass add a strong visual accent to a garden.**

THE POWER OF BIG PERENNIALS

▼ **Miscanthus framed by joe-pye weed and black-eyed susan is a useful screen as well as showy.**

Modern life is full of straight lines and rigid routines, which is one reason a garden—in which plants dominate and nature rules—refreshes the spirit. More and more designers are stressing plant-driven rather than floral-driven gardenscapes.

In these new-style gardens, bold-shape, oversize plants often play the space-defining role traditionally assigned to hardscaping (paving, walls, trellises, and arbors). But even in the smaller garden, large plants have their place, lending a surprising sense of the dramatic.

In warm climates where a wide range of true tropical plants flourish, it's easy to give

▷ **Creamy plumes of goatsbeard and white shasta daisy combine with spires of blue delephinum and pink foxglove.**

▼ **By fall, miscanthus is at full height and flowering, bridging the space between fading flowers of showy sedum and golden maples.**

any garden a lush, junglelike appearance. Gunnera and New Zealand flax grow to amazing proportions. Drier-hot climates nourish a wide range of astonishing desert plants, including dozens of spurges as well as broad-bladed grasses.

Mild-winter areas allow subtropicals and large-leaf foliage plants that can handle light frost to create the impression of abundance. In recent years, plant explorers have increased the palette available to home gardeners with dozens of more cold-hardy perennials, forms of former tropical house plants. Many of these introductions are finding their way into "tropicalismo gardens," which celebrate joyful gigantism. Characterized by a sense of exuberance, this style features sculptural

character with spunky style. Ambitious designers mingle large-scale native plants from their own regions with allies and exotics from all over the world, creating an international mix of plants that thrive together in the garden.

◀ The foliage of fingerleaf rodgersia makes a big impression in perennial borders, especially when combined with goatsbeard.

▼ Airy spires of plume poppy reach 10 feet tall, producing a dramatic late-summer show for the back border.

Big, Bold, and Beautiful

Goatsbeard *(Aruncus)*	Plume poppy *(Macleaya)*
Joe-pye weed *(Eupatorium)*	Ostrich fern *(Matteuccia)*
Gunnera *(Gunnera)*	Zebra grass *(Miscanthus)*
Hardy hibiscus *(Hibiscus)*	Fingerleaf rodgersia *(Rodgersia)*
Hosta *(Hosta)*	Culver's root *(Veronicastrum)*
Cardinal flower *(Lobelia)*	

MASTERING COLOR

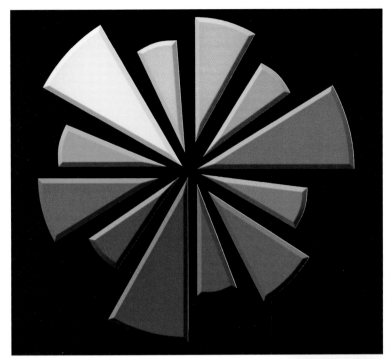

▲ Combining colors that are adjacent on a color wheel creates a harmonious scheme, while mixing those opposite one another creates drama.

Developing a theme

In choosing colors for your garden, consider the overall effect you want to achieve. Solid sheets of unbroken color work well in larger landscapes but may seem relentless in smaller gardens, especially if many of the plants remain in bloom for a long time.

It's most effective to repeat colorful vignettes—small groups of related-color plants—throughout the garden. Each vignette should have plants for each season—spring, summer, autumn, and even winter. In formal settings, space these color repetitions precisely. Cottage or naturalistic gardens, however, call for informality. Avoid a boring sameness; vary form, height, mass, and texture within each color grouping.

▼ A yellow theme established by hakone grass is punctuated by blues and lavenders.

Color brings the garden to life, and color considerations are a part of all garden designs. Flowers and foliage transform the daily greenery of gardens into a multicolor harmony. Color stimulates senses, awakens emotions, and stirs a sense of beauty. The color wheel on this page illustrates basic color compatibilities, but there are no inflexible rules because tastes are so personal. Some people like things subdued; others delight in the brazen and enjoy a brilliant clash. The bottom line is that garden color should gladden your spirit and suit your style and sensibilities.

When working with color, use your intuition and fortify it with a few techniques gleaned from artists. Painters and photographers know that light has everything to do with how you perceive color. Every flower and foliage color shifts from day to night, as the slanted light of morning becomes the floodlight of noon and then the backlight of evening. Position also matters; when light strikes plants set on a bank, it reveals undertones in the foliage, often purple or copper or burgundy, that are masked in massed bed plantings. Indirect or filtered light, such as dappled shade, brings out depths in soft colors that may be bleached in stronger light.

USING THE COLOR WHEEL

The color wheel is a device designed to show the basic interrelationships of colors. Referring to it will help in selecting your flowers and blending them in the garden. For example, red, red-orange, orange, yellow-orange, and yellow are considered warm colors; green, blue-green, blue, blue-violet, and violet are considered cool. (Red-violet and yellow-green have both warm and cool properties.)

Although colors are neither warm nor cool in a physical sense, they can impart feelings of warmth or coolness, and of passion or tranquillity. Cool colors are calming, while warm colors create instant excitement.

To the eye, warm colors tend to advance and cool colors tend to recede: If planted side by side at a distance, the warm-color plants would appear closer, the cool-color ones farther away. You can use these effects to create spatial illusions. A planting of predominantly cool-color flowers at the rear of your garden would make the yard

▲ **Multicolor blanket flower and golden tickseed are good choices wherever you want to add a feeling of warmth.**

COOL-COLOR PERENNIALS

Azure monkshood (*Aconitum*)
'Blue Fortune' anise hyssop (*Agastache*)
Rocky Mountain columbine (*Aquilegia*)
'Bluebell' peach-leaf bellflower (*Campanula*)
Delphinium (*Delphinium*)
Globe thistle (*Echinops*)
Sea holly (*Eryngium*)
Russian sage (*Perovskia*)
'Sentimental Blue' balloon flower (*Platycodon*)
'May Night' meadow salvia (*Salvia*)

WARM-COLOR PERENNIALS

Butterfly weed (*Asclepias*)
Basket-of-gold (*Aurinia*)
Strawberry foxglove (*Digitalis*)
Geum (*Geum*)
Torch lily (*Kniphofia*)
Heliopsis (*Heliopsis*)
Scarlet rose mallow (*Hibiscus*)
'Jacob Cline' bee balm (*Monarda*)
'Prairie Fire' hybrid penstemon (*Penstemon*)
'Desert Blaze' autumn sage (*Salvia*)

seem larger; warm color-plants would make it seem smaller. Spot plantings can have similar effects, seeming to deepen a part of the yard or to bring it closer.

Generally, cool colors are good for close-up viewing and warm colors better for dramatic displays. Plantings of soft blue bellflower, violet Russian sage, and clear blue balloon flower may have quite an impact next to the patio or walkway, but planted in the background of the garden they would lose their effect. To emphasize cool colors, it's best to plant them closest to the point from which they'll be most often viewed. Warm-color plants, such as scarlet rose mallow, yellow false sunflower, and orange butterfly weed, can be used to bring a distant part of the yard into sharp focus. When combining warm and cool colors, remember that the cooler colors can easily be overwhelmed by the warm.

◀ **Blues and purples in flowers of bearded iris, French lavender, and Persian onion, create a cooling effect.**

COLOR PLANNING

Simple principles of color can help greatly in selecting your flowers and blending them in the garden. A pure color is often called a hue. A tint is lighter than the pure color, and a shade is darker. In combining hues, tints, and shades, there are four basic schemes with different effects:

■ **Monochromatic schemes** are those with flowers in various tints and shades of one color. No garden is truly monochromatic, of course, because the green of foliage is always present, but a garden in tints and shades of one color can be particularly harmonious and attractive. Many gardeners use a monochromatic scheme to complement the color of the house.

▲ **Purple and white coneflowers combine with liatris spires in a monochromatic perennial garden.**

◄ **Use gardens of analogous colors, such as pink and red roses, purple geraniums, and pink foxglove to accent the color of your house.**

◄ **Combine colors opposite each other on the color wheel, such as yellow and purple, for a complementary color scheme.**

■ **Analogous schemes** use colors closely related to one another on the color wheel. Any three adjoining colors are said to be analogous, for example, red, red-violet, and violet. These schemes have been used in creating some of the world's most beautiful gardens, and can be easily reinterpreted in your own landscape.

■ **Complementary schemes** combine colors opposite one another on the wheel, for example, red and green, yellow and violet, and orange and blue. These are powerful mixes; clashing to some, vibrant and vital to others. They are best with pure hues, rather than shades or tints. If you want to try to blend strong complementary colors, arrange them to intermingle where they meet rather than be clearly defined. To tone these colors down, include silvery leaf or white-flower plants. If you want to plant intensely colored flowers, such as scarlet oriental poppies, clear yellow black-eyed susans, or hot pink New York asters, you can always lead up to the bright spots with plants of similar but less intense colors. Beds and borders designed according to this principle have a pleasing rhythm and cohesion.

■ **Polychromatic schemes** often produce a gay, carnival atmosphere in the garden. They may combine any colors and every color. These are often the result of random plantings, particularly by the novice gardener. There is nothing wrong with mixing colors. In fact, it can lead to some happy surprises—accidental but pleasing color combinations that become the mainstay of the garden for years.

COLOR FROM FOLIAGE

People often begin gardening because they fall for the flowers. But over time, their appreciation of foliage increases as well. That's not surprising given that foliage color provides the garden body and depth and can be used in the palette the same way as flower colors. And while flower colors come and go, foliage colors remain.

Perennials come with foliage in all shades and tints of green, in blue-green, blue-gray, silvery blue, silvery gray, and gray, and in many variegations. Plants with silver or gray foliage have become the favorites of many gardeners.

Silver mound artemisia, lamb's-ears, and mullein are just some of the silver- or gray-foliage plants that have striking effects when combined with flowers, particularly white flowers or blooms in the pale blue to lavender range of the spectrum. When planted adjacent to hot colors, silver-leaf plants will cool them down.

Beyond green foliage

In addition to the multitude of greens are the perennials with purple, red, bronze, golden, and yellow foliage. Strikingly beautiful gardens with vivid contrasts can be made by combining these colors with green-foliaged plants. Purple foliage from perennials adds weight and balance to a scheme, while yellow and gold brighten and warm up an area. Yellow-leaf plants, such as 'Aureola' golden hakone grass, are compatible with purple-leaf plants, including many of the coral bells, and those with blue and purple flowers.

Using variegation

Perennials with variegated leaves offer a variety of color combinations and endless patterns—from speckles and spots to stripes and blotches. They can lend focus to a jumble and elevate a dull planting to high art. But they may also create visual chaos if overused.

Treat them as jewels, sparingly, to lighten the garden tapestry and illuminate dark spaces. For harmonious color combinations, pick up one color in the variegated leaf and choose companion plants that echo that color. If you're concerned about your vignettes becoming busy, include simple patterns—perhaps an edging of cream or pink or yellow—and combine these plants with perennials that have large, simple green leaves.

▶ Silvery stems and leaves of lamb's-ears add color and interest to the garden from spring to fall.

▽ Yellow-leaf moneywort combines beautifully with purple-leaf coral bells and blue-flowering catmint.

TOP VARIEGATED PERENNIALS

Japanese painted fern *(Athyrium)*
'Looking Glass' brunnera *(Brunnera)*
'Ruby Veil' coral bells *(Heuchera)*
'Great Expectations' hosta *(Hosta)*
'Herman's Pride' yellow archangel *(Lamiastrum)*
'Morning Light' miscanthus *(Miscanthus)*
Variegated solomon's seal *(Polygonatum)*
'Excalibur' lungwort *(Pulmonaria)*

▶ Cream and white-stripe leaves of sweet iris contribute color and light to the garden before and after flowers.

Choosing And Growing Perennials

Walk into your yard and look around. Get an image of the existing landscape. Take photographs of it from various points of view that you can study later. Reviewing images at a later time, in a different context, often helps reveal aspects of the scene that are more difficult to see in person.

Notice problem areas where nothing seems to grow but weeds, or where the soil is perpetually soggy. Also note any less-than-pleasing view, such as the one that includes your neighbors' trash barrels. The importance of completing this basic inventory can't be overstated. It's likely you'll learn as much about your yard as you will glean useful details for planning your vision of a garden.

Families and their gardens change and evolve over time. Small children grow up and move away, or perhaps grandparents move in. Reflecting on your changing situation, needs, and interests, in combination with a careful study of your existing garden, is where to begin.

You can successfully grow perennials in nearly every gardening situation that you can imagine. But the key is matching the right plant to the right place. Even the most difficult problem areas are opportunities that can become beautiful gardens given good plant choices. Matched to a compatible site, your perennials will grow well, bloom readily, and more than likely successfully fend off pests.

Shop for plants at your local home or garden center, or for hard to find plants, by mail. As you browse, take notes and maybe digital snapshots, then peruse the Perennials Selection Guide starting on page 52, and soon you will have the makings of a plant list for your garden.

▶ Perennials can serve utilitarian as well as aesthetic functions. What was sloping lawn is now a perennial garden. Plants such as bearded iris, salvia, and centranthus, and false indigo knit together the grade changes made by the retaining walls. Note also how the elevation changes create a natural layering, or tiers, of perennials. Naturally low-growing plants bloom at eye level.

MATCHING PLANTS TO THE SITE

▲ From a plant's point of view, the most important characteristic of the garden may be its annual temperature range. Snow fails to faze a lenten rose.

W hich perennials will grow best for you depends in large part upon your region and its climate. Climate, in fact, may be the single most decisive factor in your gardening plan.

Before you purchase your perennials, this much research is essential: You need to know the cold and heat hardiness zone for your region (see the maps on page 122 and 123). If a plant is listed in a catalog or in the Perennials Selection Guide (pages 52 to 121) as hardy to your area, that means it is likely to survive both winters and summers where you live.

Cold hardiness, however, is only one aspect of climate. A plant listed as hardy to Zone 8, for example, will survive winters in both Atlanta and Portland, Oregon. However, it may thrive in a Portland summer but wilt in Atlanta's. Some sources, including the Perennials Selection Guide,

▼ Where a microclimate in your yard creates an environment that's warmer or colder than normal, choose plants that can take advantage of that difference.

will list hardiness zones in a range. If your favorite perennial choices are designated as hardy in Zones 4 to 7, for example, they will survive winters in Zone 4 (and regions that are warmer) and generally do well in summers in Zone 7 (and cooler).

Within zones, there are considerations other than temperature. The high humidity of the South, for example, can be as challenging to perennials as the heat. So can clay or sandy soils. Humidity invites some insects and diseases, and extreme soil conditions can cause plants to get too much or too little water. You can, however, choose perennials that adapt to these conditions.

In the Southwest, the dry air and soil challenge many plants. Rainfall is relatively sparse, and watering times for gardens may be restricted on occasion. But again, there are many plants perfectly suited to these conditions.

Likewise, many perennials can survive northern winters. In fact, these hardy perennials are extremely cold tolerant and are also among the first plants to bloom in spring.

Take stock of your garden's unique environments. These microclimates are small pockets where temperatures, light, soil, and drainage are distinctly different.

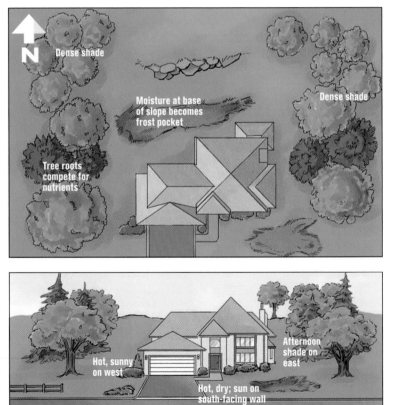

Dense shade

Moisture at base of slope becomes frost pocket

Dense shade

Tree roots compete for nutrients

Dry and windy at top of slope

Partial shade

Hot, sunny on west

Afternoon shade on east

Hot, dry; sun on south-facing wall

MICROCLIMATES

◄ Yellow flag iris, pink Japanese primrose, fingerleaf rodgersia, and siebold hosta are among the perennials that thrive in boggy, wet soil.

▲ Dry, baking slopes are notorious for the gardening challenges they present. But perennials such as centranthus, dianthus, salvia, thyme, and veronica thrive in these conditions.

▼ Many kinds of perennials, such as hosta, lungwort, and meadow rue, can thrive and flower in the shade cast by tall trees.

Microclimates put a kink into the broad generalizations about hardiness. When choosing plants for these places, you'll want to account for differences.

Microclimates are small areas where the soil and climate differ from surrounding areas; they are created by any number of conditions. For instance, the slope of the ground and the lay of the land channel cold air. That air accumulates, like water, in low spots. This is why the base of hills and other low-lying areas may be more prone to frost than the rest of your yard. In fact, these areas may be cold enough that you need to plant a perennial that is a zone hardier. Water also runs down slopes, and the bases of slopes are usually wet. At the same time, the tops of hills and slopes may be drier and warmer than other areas. An open area might be exposed to more wind than other locations. Places shaded by trees, shrubs, or the shadow of the house may stay cooler.

Orientation to the sun also affects soil and air temperatures. In the northern hemisphere, a window or garden bed directly exposed to the south and west is warmer than areas facing north and east.

Buildings and structures of all kinds affect microclimates. For instance, plants in beds adjacent to a south-facing concrete wall benefit at night from the heat stored during the day, and likewise may suffer from too much heat during daytime hours. Similarly, beds adjacent to the house in a cold climate will benefit from the warmth of that wall. In Zone 4, planting adjacent to the house might allow the survival of Zone 5 plants to survive. However, structures influence plants in other ways. The soil next to a building with a concrete foundation is likely to be more alkaline than native soil because of the calcium in the concrete.

You can also indentify microclimates by observing existing plants. Plants may seem more lush or productive in some spots, while only certain plants flourish in others. Discrepancies in plant growth are signs of different growing conditions.

SOIL BASICS

▶ Squeezing a handful of moist soil can tell you a a great deal about your soil's texture. The ideal loam soil is a mixture of sand, silt, and clay particles in a proportion that is favorable to the root growth of most perennials.

The future success of your plants depends on developing healthy roots. That's why it's important to make the soil around the roots the best it can be. Most perennials grow fast, sturdy, and healthy in loose, well-drained, weed-free, fertile loam with a pH of about 6.5 (see the box at right). Before planting, figure out which of these characteristics your soil might lack, then fix it.

It's best to amend soil in fall. Preparing soil then allows time for the soil-enhancing activity of worms, frost, and rain to supplement your work; amendments to make their changes; and the soil to settle so it is ready for planting. But whatever time of year you choose, make sure the soil is friable. Squeeze a handful of soil, then open your hand. The soil should not ooze water, and it should readily crumble.

Plants need drainage

Roots need both moisture and air to grow properly, and soils that are either excessively wet or dry inhibit root growth. Hence, developing soil that permits water and air to easily move into and through it is the single best way for the gardener to ensure plant success. Water flows into soil pores, drawing air behind it. A well-drained soil has much in common with a moist sponge, and even feels similar to it.

There are various causes for excessively wet or dry soils, but the most common is native soil texture. Soils composed primarily of very fine particles, called clays, tend to pack tightly and restrict circulation of water and air. At the opposite end of the spectrum, soils composed of relatively large particles, called sands, allow water and air to enter and exit too easily and tend to be too dry. Most soils combine clay and sand in varying proportions, and the one most ideal for plants is called loam.

The way to improve either a clay or sandy soil is with organic matter, both by incorporating it into the soil and, after planting, by using it to mulch the soil around plants. Organic matter, both

▶ Check the natural drainage of your soil by digging an 18-inch-deep hole and filling it with water. Wait until it drains completely and then refill it. If the hole drains within 3½ hours, your soil is fast-draining. If it takes up to 24 hours, your soil is well drained. But if your soil needs more than 24 hours to empty, you should take steps to improve the rate of drainage.

initially and as it decomposes, modifies how soil particles interact, making management simpler and more successful.

Soil fertility

Soil fertility is a measure of a soil's ability to support plant growth and hold nutrients. A soil test, conducted by a university or commercial laboratory, is the best way to learn about the fertility of your soil and decide on specific steps to take to improve it. Another is simple observation: Are other plants or weeds in the area growing well, or not? When you turn over a shovelful of soil, do you see earthworms? The vigorous growth of surrounding plants and the presence of earthworms in the soil are both indications of healthy, fertile soil.

Too much fertilizer is as big a problem as too little, which is why testing soil is so beneficial, especially when you're just getting started. But if you determine without a test that your soil needs fertilizer, mix in up to ½ pound of a general purpose 10-10-10 fertilizer or ¼ pound of 20-20-20 fertilizer for every 100 square feet of bed as you prepare the garden. (The three numbers are required by law on all fertilizers, and specify the proportions of nitrogen, phosphorous, and potassium in the bag by weight.) Rake it lightly into the top few inches of the soil. The granules will dissolve and spread downward, ensuring that equal amounts of nitrogen, phosphorus, and potassium reach the soil the first season.

Improving soil structure

Loam is considered ideal because it has enough clay particles to be fertile and adequate large sand particles to drain quickly and warm up early in spring.

Your soil may have an imbalance of sand, silt, or clay, which can cause problems. For example, excess clay makes for a sticky soil through which water and nutrients are slow to move. Sandy soil retains less moisture and fewer nutrients than clay or loamy soils. In such situations, gardeners often focus on changing their soil's texture. But improving the structure (the way individual soil particles bind together) is a more practical way to improve plant growth, and structure is easier to change than texture.

To improve soil structure, add organic matter at every opportunity. Microorganisms feed on the organic matter and produce a glue that coats mineral particles and causes them to stick together in granules that retain moisture, air, and nutrients. Till or turn organic matter or compost into the soil as you prepare the bed, or add it by sheet composting (a surface layer of organic matter). Use a 2- to 3-inch layer of moistened compost, or a 3- to 4-inch layer of chopped leaves.

SOIL PREPARATION

◀ Improving the soil before planting is a smart investment. Your plants will be healthier and better looking, and they will need less maintenance.

Once you've established your soil conditions and determined which amendments are needed, the next step is to prepare the soil for planting.

Many soils need cultivating and amending because they're dense or compacted from foot traffic, grading, or seasonal flooding. As an example, just eight passes with a bulldozer during construction or relandscaping work can reduce the ideal 50 percent air and water space in a soil to only 5 to 10 percent. Kids' play can be nearly as hard on the soil.

Perennials grow best in beds with loose soil that is at least 18 inches deep, but you need dig only as deep as necessary to loosen the layer of compacted soil, if it exists. Sometimes only the top few inches of soil may be dense. But it is also common to find a compacted layer several inches below the surface under relatively loose soil. This deeper compaction may exist because your proposed garden used to be farmland or a vegetable garden repeatedly tilled to that depth.

If you can reach into your soil with your bare hands, it's perfect. If you must soak it before digging or if you need to use a pickax to make a hole, it needs serious work. You can loosen soil by hand digging or you can use a tiller.

■ **Hand cultivation:** Use a spade or spading fork (a fork's tines are better at penetrating dense soil) to cut, lift, or turn soil. Manual loosening works best in small areas; in weedy areas where each square foot of soil must be inspected and cleared of weed roots; in existing beds between established plants and tree roots; and in soil that must be loosened deeper than a tiller's 6- to 8-inch blades can reach.

Single-dig to loosen well-drained loam. Double-dig to break up hardpan (a layer of soil densely packed by machinery or traffic, preventing the free flow of water and air) or to loosen soil 18 inches deep, if necessary. (See the illustrations below.)

■ **Power cultivation:** As tillers slice, lift, cut, and drop soil in chunks, they increase the amount of air between clods. But using one is practical only in a large garden, free of perennial weeds and tree roots. Full-size tillers are hard to maneuver in small areas;

▶ **Single-digging:** Use a spade or spading fork to loosen the top 8 to 10 inches of soil. Insert the fork to its full depth and pull back on the handle to lever the tines through the soil.

▲ **Double-digging:** Make a 9-inch-deep trench across the bed, stockpiling soil on a tarp. With a fork, loosen the trench's bottom to 9 inches deep; top with compost. Dig a second trench alongside, tossing its soil into the first. Loosen, add compost, and continue to the end of the bed. Fill the last trench with the set-aside soil. Rake to level, allowing for some settling, and avoid standing on the loosened soil.

tree roots are damaged by tines; and some perennial weeds multiply when their roots are chopped. Use a much smaller minitiller, also called a power cultivator, to turn the soil in raised beds and small areas.

Avoid excess tilling or working in wet soil. Soil that is churned too often by a tiller or shovel loses structure, becoming similar to sifted flour. Till only enough to turn, not pulverize. Repeated tilling to the same depth can also create a layer of hardpan; check every few years to see whether hardpan is developing at the 6- to 8-inch depth. Similarly, shoveling or tilling wet clay soil forces air out and turns the soil into a concretelike slurry. Both conditions make it more difficult for air and water to move through the soil.

▌Adding amendments: When you turn or till the soil, it's also a good time to add materials to help prevent future compaction. Use porous substances that don't crush easily, are long-lasting, and have relatively large particles. Examples of good soil amendments include composted fir or pine bark or other high-quality compost. Inorganic amendments to add include those that modify the soil's pH, such as dolomitic limestone or soil sulfur. Before turning or tilling, spread amendments over the area in a 2- to 3-inch layer and mix them into the entire depth of soil that needs loosening.

Good soil amendments make two important contributions: They physically create more open spaces for air and water circulation and drainage, and they also

▲ **Till amendments such as compost into a new garden bed, working in the material until there are no distinct layers.**

gradually increase fertility. For instance, as compost continues to decompose in the soil, it forms other materials, such as humic acids, that act like magnets to soil particles. Grains of clay and sand gradually attach themselves to humic acids, which alters soil structure for the better.

▼ **A power tiller is a convenient way to work amendment into soil over a large area.**

PLANTING

▶ To see your planting plan on the ground before committing to it, lay out your plants and then double-check against the planting plan.

You can plant perennials any time of year that the soil is workable, but they make the strongest start if planted when the air is cool and the soil warm and moist. Cool air retards top growth while moist, warm soil stimulates rooting, allowing plants to establish wide, drought-resistant, stem-stabilizing roots.

In northern regions, the best times to plant are midspring and early autumn before leaf fall. In the South and West, fall is the preferred planting time. Again, the air is cool, but the soil is still warm. Plants will benefit from the winter rains and roots will be well established before the challenges of the next summer.

Overcast and drizzly days are ideal for planting. Avoid the middle of a hot day, when water from leaves is lost more quickly than it can be replaced. Even if no permanent damage is done, recovering from wilt takes time and consumes energy that the plant could have used to develop roots into the new site.

▲ Because most root growth occurs nearer the oxygen-rich surface of the soil, it makes sense to dig a wide hole with sloped sides.

HOW MANY PLANTS TO BUY?

The number of plants that will fit into your garden depends on the garden's square footage (sq. ft.) and how far apart the plants should be from one another. Because perennial gardens are generally filled with plants having varying spacing requirements, you may find it helpful to measure the area allotted for each clump individually. The chart lists three common-size gardens and eight plant spacings. To determine the number of plants to buy for your garden, estimate the square footage of your garden and plant spacing you will use in it.

Spacing (inches)	30 sq. ft.	100 sq. ft.	170 sq. ft.
4	270	900	1530
6	120	400	680
8	68	225	383
10	44	144	245
12	30	100	170
15	19	64	109
18	14	45	76
24	8	25	43

Hardening before planting

Perennials grown in a greenhouse without wind, wide temperature fluctuations, or direct sun need time to adjust to different, harsher conditions. This process is called hardening.

Not every perennial requires hardening. But plants that have been in a dark package in the mail and those sold from inside a greenhouse in early spring are not ready to be planted. When buying perennials from an outdoor sales area, ask whether they have been hardened or simply moved out each day from indoors.

To harden plants, place them outdoors in a spot protected from the wind and out of the midday sun for several days. At night, cover them to protect them from rapid cooling or move them into a protected area—near the house or in a shed, for example. Gradually give the plants slightly longer exposure to outdoor conditions for about a week. At that time they will be fully adjusted to outdoor conditions.

Plant spacing

Before digging, use one of these techniques to visualize the garden and make changes before planting: Set the perennials in the bed while still in their containers, or use stakes to mark the place in the bed where each plant will grow. This way it is simple to make any final adjustments. Some gardeners use markers of various colors and heights to match the expected show. You might use bonemeal or flour to outline locations of plant groups. And before planting, double-check mature height and spread.

Handling root balls

Handle the root ball carefully as you remove it from the pot. Avoid lifting a plant out of the pot by pulling on its stems. Instead, invert the pot, support the soil on your spread fingers or hands, and lift the pot off the root ball.

If a plant will not slide out easily, rap the inverted pot sharply on its rim while supporting the weight of the soil. If a container is flexible, roll it on a hard surface to separate the root mass from the pot, or cut the pot away from the root mass.

If you discover that a purchased container plant is rootbound, prune the roots slightly. Otherwise, the roots will probably grow only from the bottom of the root ball. Slice off the bottom layer of roots and score the sides vertically in several places. After taking time to repair its injuries, the plant will develop new roots at each point where the roots were severed.

Planting width and depth

Make planting holes wider at the top and tapering with depth; most new root growth will occur close to the soil's surface. Adjust the depth of the planting hole so the perennial is at the same level as it was in the pot or field. With few exceptions, setting perennials too deep invites crown-rot problems. Planting too high (so the root ball's shoulders are aboveground) can cause problems: Moisture will wick from the roots into the air, checking root growth.

Watering after planting

Plants will root best if both the original root ball and the earth around it stay moist throughout the first growing season. Build a watering basin to trap and hold rain and irrigation so water soaks into that vital area. About 2 to 3 inches beyond the root ball or farthest spread root, scrape excess or leftover excavated soil into a circular levee about 1 or 2 inches high around the entire perennial. Fill the basin each time you water, and it will direct a full ration of water to the roots below.

◀ With the planting hole ready, slide the root ball carefully out of the pot. Some root balls are not fully knitted into a tight mass and could be easily damaged.

▶ Set the plant in the hole and check planting height. Adjust the depth of the hole by either excavating more soil or adding some back in until the plant sits at the same level as it did in its pot.

◀ Build a water-holding basin around the plant and directly over the root ball. Water gently so the basin and backfill soil aren't washed away, though some repairs will probably be necessary within the first few days after planting.

MULCHING

A ll plantings profit from mulch, which is, technically, just about any material that blankets the ground. In practice, most mulches are organic material, mimicking the natural mulch found on a forest floor.

Mulching has a host of benefits, including keeping the bed clean. It prevents rapid heating or cooling of the soil, thereby allowing steadier root growth. It reduces water loss to evaporation. If an organic material is used as mulch, its particles become soil-enriching humus as they decompose. In addition, well-chosen mulch with a color and texture that is complementary to the perennials becomes a landscape element itself, making the whole bed more attractive.

Apply a blanket of mulch to cover the entire bed, including watering craters, but leave a bare ring an inch or two out from the crown of each perennial. Mulch resting against perennials' stems can trap moisture and rot the stems.

▲ **Mulch is nearly as integral to a perennial garden as the plants themselves. It will serve many needed functions, and make the garden look good, too.**

▶ **Cover the root area with mulch, but avoid piling it around the plant's main stem.**

Spread woody mulch, such as bark or composted ground wood, 2 to 3 inches deep. Spread leafy mulches and hulls, such as shredded leaves, pine straw, cocoa hulls, rice hulls, and nut shells, 2 to 4 inches deep.

Mulch materials

Many materials can be used as mulch. Select one that has a color and texture you prefer, is readily available, and fits your garden budget. Also consider scent—some people like the odor of ground fir bark or cocoa hulls; others don't.

The best perennial mulches are organic materials that will decompose between 12 and 18 months after application. Once broken down into earthy-scented, unrecognizable dark crumbs, they can be allowed to mix into the soil during the normal course of garden activities.

Mulches that decompose more rapidly, such as grass clippings, must be renewed as the mulch layer becomes thin and weed seeds begin to sprout. If the initial pile is too deep, fresh grass clippings will rot to a slimy mess, then dry into a water-shedding, cardboardlike mat. Spread new clippings no more than 2 inches deep; they'll dry without matting. Once they've dried, you can put another layer on top of the first.

Mulches that decompose more slowly or not at all, such as rocks, may cause extra work for the gardener when dividing perennials, fertilizing, or weeding. Those mulches must be moved out of the way and put back later so they do not mix with the soil as you work.

Mulch	Properties*	Other notes
Shredded, chipped, or processed bark	Brown; darkness varies; smallest particle size tends to be darkest, but widely variable so look before you buy if color matters. Coarse to fine in texture, widely variable. Uses nitrogen as it decomposes and could intercept fertilizer applied to plants; little effect on pH.	All bark and wood products may bring slime mold with them; it is rarely harmful but is unsightly. Use products with small chunks. Large chunks get in the way whenever you need to disturb the soil, are slow to decompose, and attract slugs.
Chipped wood	Gray-white to light brown; often fades to much paler color. Medium texture. Uses lots of nitrogen as it decomposes; little effect on pH.	Not recommended. May consist of recycled wood colored with vegetable dye, which leaches. Wood containing copper or arsenic, such as pressure-treated lumber, may have herbicidal properties.
Sawdust	Yellow to white; fine texture. Uses lots of nitrogen as it decomposes; little effect on pH.	Cultivate regularly; otherwise fungal strands can web particles together and block water absorption.
Hulls: cocoa bean, nut, buckwheat, rice	Color and texture vary. Often supply nutrients as they decompose. Less likely to tie up nitrogen than wood products; neutral to acidifying effect on pH.	Availability varies.
Residue: spent hops, ground corncob	Color and texture vary. May supply nutrients as it decomposes; neutral to acidifying effect on soil pH.	Acquaint yourself with the odor of these mulches before selecting one.
Yard waste, compost, spent mushroom compost	Very dark brown to black-brown; fine texture. May supply nutrients. Neutral to alkaline effect on pH.	Test pH and soluble salts. Extremely alkaline compost with high-soluble salts is common and may stunt perennial growth. Check cleanliness by sifting for pieces of weed roots; then fill a pot with compost, moisten it, and watch for weed seedlings.
Leaves: deciduous tree leaves or pine needles	Color varies from light brown to yellow; texture varies. Supply nutrients as they decompose; neutral to acidifying effect on pH.	May include tree and weed seeds. Appearance is best if shredded; large, slow-decaying leaves such as sycamore, oak, and Norway maple can mat unless shredded. Pine needles can be slippery underfoot.
Stones	Color and texture vary. Rarely supply nutrients. Limestone increases pH.	Not recommended among perennials because they get in the way whenever you need to disturb the soil.
Chicken grit	Gray color; fine texture. No nutrient value. Little effect on pH.	Use for perennials intolerant of moist soil pressing against foliage or crown, or for windy and rooftop beds where lighter mulches may blow away.
Ceramic soil conditioner	Gray-brown color; medium texture. No effect on nutrients or pH.	Use for perennials intolerant of moist soil against foliage or crown, or for windy and rooftop beds where lighter mulches may blow away.
Shredded paper	Color varies; medium texture. Little effect on nutrients. No effect on pH.	Low cost. Avoid use of glossy paper, which could contain toxic inks. Often unattractive and should be covered by a more attractive mulch.
Grass clippings	Pale green to straw color; fine texture. High in nitrogen. Little effect on pH.	Low cost. Apply cool and fresh from mower bag. Must renew more often than most. May contain weed seeds. Avoid using clippings sprayed with weed killer within two weeks of mowing.
Cones, spruce or pine	Color varies; coarse texture. Insignificant effect on nutrients or pH.	Economical way to recycle materials. Low cost where conifers are abundant.
Spent soilless potting mix from patio containers	Dark brown; fine texture. No effect on nutrient levels. Acidifying effect on pH.	May promote weed growth.
Coffee grounds, eggshells, other food-preparation castoffs	Color and texture vary. May supply nutrients. Some materials are acidifying, others mildly alkaline.	Economical way to recycle materials. Ask at coffee shops and office building coffee stations about obtaining coffee grounds.

*Dark brown to black-brown colors work well with the widest range of perennial foliage and flowers; fine-textured mulches with a smooth appearance are the most complementary. For overly acidic or alkaline soil, avoid mulches that raise or lower pH.

WATERING

Fast-growing perennials need an average of 1 to 2 inches of water a week, whether from rain or supplemental sources. How do you know if you apply that much?

To measure the output of a sprinkler, let it fill a rain gauge to the 1-inch mark, or use a straight-sided container, such as a tuna can. Filling may take 15 minutes to 6 hours, depending on water pressure, hose length, sprinkler type, size of area, wind, and evaporation rate.

To measure the output of a drip or weeper line, check the soil 1 foot from an emitter or the far end of the hose. One inch of water wets clay soil to a depth of 3 to 4 inches and sandy soil to a depth of 18 inches. Dig down that far with a shovel. If the soil feels cool or moist at that level, it has received water. It will take several hours to apply 1 inch of water through a drip system or weeper hose.

▲ Most perennials need about an inch of water a week. If your region doesn't naturally supply that much in rain, look to drought-tolerant plants.

Understand the site

No garden is so uniform in either soil or exposure that all parts are either moist or dry at once. There are always areas where soil retains moisture longer and others that dry faster. With experience you'll learn to watch for those areas that dry first and to use them as indicators of when to water.

Several factors affect how often you water and the technique you use.

■ **Rain:** Monitor weather reports or check the rain gauge, then water each week to make up the difference. In large beds, use several rain gauges to ensure that all plantings receive adequate water.

■ **Soil type:** One inch of water may keep clay moist for more than a week, but excessively drained sandy soils may need frequent light waterings totaling more than 1 inch a week.

■ **Soil condition:** Infiltration rate—how quickly moisture seeps into soil pores—may be slow on compacted soil and on slopes. Some silty soils repel water when they're dry. Compensate by watering slowly, or water in cycles, stopping when the water begins to run off and restarting after it soaks in. Use organic mulch. The mulch helps retain water, preventing runoff.

■ **Plants:** Some perennials wilt rapidly when the soil moisture is low; others like it dry. Most fall somewhere in between. For easy maintenance, group perennials by their particular watering needs.

▼ When watering with a portable sprinkler, watch to make sure that you're not losing water to runoff.

Critical watering times

New plants dry out more quickly than perennials with wide, established root systems. Regularly check newly planted perennials during the first season, with watering can in hand.

Plants need water most when they are growing rapidly. A week of summer drought may cause no lasting problem, compared with the season-long effect of a momentary one in springtime.

It's important to water in fall, when perennials aren't growing many leaves but are sending out roots. Moisture in fall can greatly improve the next year's show.

Water in the early morning for the best results. At first light, the air is calm and during the day plants take up water rapidly so there's little waste. The foliage dries quickly as the air warms and breezes stir. This also thwarts leaf diseases that thrive on damp leaves and high humidity.

There are exceptions to morning irrigation. In hot, dry regions where water is scarce, nighttime irrigation reduces the amount of water lost to evaporation. The risk of infection is not significant, because humidity-loving leaf diseases are suppressed by extremely dry air.

Some plants, especially recent transplants, may need midday watering to cool the air and prevent wilt. You might water frequently if you're helping certain plants recover from stress, such as heavy insect infestation or hailstorm damage.

Ways to water

Choose the watering system—overhead or direct-to-soil, automatic or manual—suited to the site and your needs.

Overhead systems cleanse foliage, keeping dust-related problems and mite damage low. Their output is easily measured, and the systems are readily available in many forms. But your plants are at increased risk of leaf diseases and battered foliage if plants grow across a spray path, and runoff can be a problem.

Direct-to-soil watering conserves water and keeps foliage dry, but you may have difficulty measuring amounts applied or remembering to be vigilant with drip lines and weepers. In such invisible flows, clogs can go unnoticed until plants that are downstream wilt.

▲ **Wherever most garden moisture is supplied by irrigation and not rainfall, consider using efficient drip or microspray watering systems.**

An automatic system frees you from wrestling with hoses. But it also may lull you into checking soil moisture less often. Overwatering and dry corners could go unnoticed.

A manual system with overhead and direct-to-soil elements plus semiautomatic extras may be best for perennials. Most botanical gardens employ these hybrid systems in perennial areas.

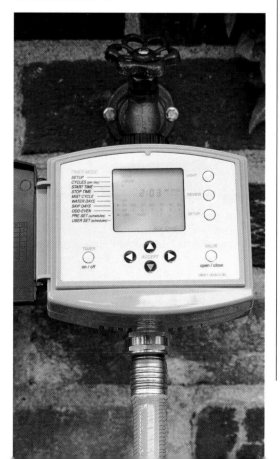

▶ **An oscillating overhead sprinkler often applies water unevenly to perennial beds. Tall plants block the spray and create dry pockets on the side opposite the water source.**

◀ **Battery-powered timers that connect between the spigot and hose are a convenient way to control portable hose-end sprinklers.**

FERTILIZING

Just as you can't rely solely on rainfall for the best perennial show, you can't expect nature to supply all the nutrients perennials require. With help, perennials will produce larger flowers, fuller foliage, and greater stature. Gardens are not natural; weeding, watering, deadheading, cutting flowers, and removing plant debris all disrupt plants' natural recycling of nutrients.

EXCEPTIONS TO THE RULES

Some perennial species grow best in lean soil, which is low in nitrogen. Others are heavy feeders and require more than average amounts of nitrogen. The following are among the more common perennials with differing needs:

HEAVY FEEDERS	LIGHT FEEDERS
Astilbe	Artemisia
Delphinium	Barrenwort
Peony	Mullein

Pale older leaves (lower ones), smaller-than-normal leaves, and thin stems indicate nitrogen need.	Weak stems, reduced flowering, and rank growth may indicate too much nitrogen has been applied near the plants.

Plants create their own food using primarily carbon dioxide, water, and sunlight. Growth and flowering are controlled by temperature, sunlight, water, and internally produced hormones.

Fertilizers provide the essential mineral elements that plants need and that they obtain from soil. The element needed in greatest quantity is nitrogen; phosphorous and potassium rank second and third. These and other elements act similar to vitamins, allowing plants to synthesize enzymes and fueling photosynthesis as well as other key metabolic processes.

Generally, to ensure essential elements are available, fertilize when perennials first start growing each year and again when flower buds begin to form. Ideally, you would fertilize each plant on its own schedule, because each species starts to grow and flower at different times—cool-season perennials first, later-emerging species weeks or months later. However, most gardens contain dozens of species and fertilizing plants individually is impossible. So the best compromise is to fertilize to meet average growth and blooming peaks.

Roots have no teeth and so can't chew fertilizer pellets or bits of rock phosphate. The only nutrient a root can use is one that is dissolved in water and in the appropriate chemical form. Generally, fertilizers

◄ Fertilizer alone cannot transform a garden. But the best perennial gardens can only develop in soil that provides all of the nutrients your plants need.

applied in solution, or that quickly go into solution with soil moisture, are more readily accessible to plant roots. But those fertilizers may leach away from the root zone as rain and irrigation water move through soil. Therefore, these materials need to be applied frequently and in small doses.

Controlled-release fertilizers supply elements over a long period. These materials include pelleted or beadlike sulfur- and polymer-coated urea products that release nutrients at predictable rates, usually according to soil moisture, temperature, or both. Apply them in late winter or early spring, just before the plants' needs are greatest.

Organic materials, such as compost, manure, or fish meal, usually release the nutrients they contain faster when soil temperatures are higher and slower when soil temperatures are lower. But because release of the nutrients they contain depends on subtle characteristics of the soil, the rate is not predictable. On the other hand, they stimulate the growth of soil microorganisms that are beneficial to plants in myriad ways. Apply organic fertilizers in late fall so nutrients will be available by spring.

Choosing a fertilizer

A soil test is the best way to know which nutrients are available in your soil and which ones and how much to add. To learn where to have your soil tested and how to prepare a sample, check with your county extension service, or search the Internet for private soil testing laboratories using the term "soil testing".

How much fertilizer

The average perennial fares well if its bed is fertilized so that ½ pound of actual nitrogen is spread over about 500 square feet. A bag of 10-10-10 fertilizer contains 10 percent nitrogen, so 5 pounds of that fertilizer is the right amount to work into 500 square feet of bed. Here's how it's figured: 10 percent (.10) multiplied by 5 pounds equals 0.5 or ½ pound of nitrogen.

Applying fertilizers

Because fertilizer must dissolve to be of use to plants, mix water-soluble types in water. Spread granular and controlled-release products over moist soil, cultivate lightly, and then water.

◀ Lightly cultivate fertilizer granules into the soil, but as you do, be careful to avoid damaging the many delicate surface roots surrounding plants.

▼ A variety of hose-end sprayers are available, all of which automatically dilute a fertilizer concentrate into the hose stream, allowing you to water and fertilize at the same time.

GROOMING

Grooming is a light but constant growing-season chore. By removing spent flowers and damaged or browning foliage on a daily or weekly basis, you help maximize flowering, keep the garden pleasantly tidy and, importantly, keep yourself aware of subtle changes in the garden.

There are two main grooming practices—in addition to general maintenance—and each has its own purpose.

■ **Deadheading.** This means removing flowers as they fade but before seeds begin to ripen, stimulating long and repeated bloom in many perennials by signaling waiting flower buds to grow. In general, cut the flower stems back to the next set of leaves; that's where the side shoots and buds will make new blooms. Use garden scissors or pruning shears to deadhead.

A perennial might double or triple its bloom frequency if regularly deadheaded. But even if plants don't respond with more flowers, the practice is worthwhile. Removing spent petals and stems gives a garden a fresh look. It also eliminates old tissue where diseases can gain a foothold on otherwise healthy plants.

Occasions when deadheading is not desirable are rare but notable. Generally do not deadhead late in the season as plants are preparing for winter. Ripening seeds trigger related processes that prepare the plant for dormancy and the capacity to withstand the rigors of winter. Another reason to leave seedheads is that many songbirds relish the seeds and fruits of garden plants. Leaving seedheads may increase the number of birds that visit.

▷ **Remove leggy, worn-out stems of catmint by cutting them off at ground level in order to make room for new growth.**

▲ **Catmint grows more lush and reblooms when old flowering stems are cut to near ground level.**

◁ **Most grooming is just cleaning up, removing faded or damaged flowers, or damaged leaves or stems. When you're through, the plant should look a little sharper.**

■ **Cutting back.** Cutting or lopping off leaves, flowers, or stems stimulates production of new stems and leaves. It removes much or all of a plant's foliage in one step. Do this when a perennial's flower production has fallen off for the season. As each stalk blooms out, cut it to the ground or to a point where new growth is evident.

Cutting back hard takes all the stalks at once, removing most or all of the plant's foliage in one day. This is done most often to perennials that grow quickly, bloom before summer's heat, or tend to cease vegetative growth once seeds begin to ripen. It eliminates tired foliage and encourages the plant to replace it with fresh green leaves, which makes the whole plant look better.

Cutting back hard is a shock to a plant, so take care which perennials you do this to. Spare newly planted, stressed, or slow growing perennials. For instance, though coreopsis is a candidate for cutting back hard, stick with simple deadheading if your plant suffered deer browsing or you transplanted it in the current season.

Supporting tall perennials

Certain perennials routinely need support if their tall or heavy flowers are to remain upright. Stakes work well for those with tall, single flower stems, such as foxglove and delphinium. Bushy, multistem perennials with lots of heavy flower heads, such as Chinese peonies and oriental poppies, may be best served by grow-through supports or cages rather than individual stakes. Sometimes the garden setting creates the need for staking plants that are otherwise sturdy. Examples are yarrow in an overrich soil, or tall perennials such as joe-pye weed in a windy location.

Install stakes or cages in early spring so you can place them close to stems without damaging the plant or roots. The supports might look awkward at first, but perennials grow so quickly from midspring to early summer that they rapidly cloak the stakes with foliage.

▶ Support the tall flowering stems of plants such as liatris with a ring-type hoop that surrounds only the stems.

▼ A large hoop with cross supports is one of the best ways to support multistem plants such as southern lupine or peony.

There are many kinds of perennial stakes and cages as well as a variety of natural materials, such as branches cut from shrubs and trees. Whatever type you use, avoid tying the plant too tightly. Motion is important in plant growth. Cell walls become stronger when the stems are occasionally jostled by wind. Use wide, straplike ties rather than thin, stringy material to hold stems; the latter is likely to pinch or snap the stem it binds. Avoid wire, coated-wire twist ties, and fishing line. Don't be stingy—use several ties for each stem to distribute the weight.

DIVIDING

◄ **Probe around the plant to find the edges of the root ball, and once you do, lift the entire root ball out of the soil.**

Dividing perennials is the easiest way to propagate new plants and is an important step in managing established plants.

Even with the cutting you do to groom perennials, they'll still produce more than enough energy for next year. This season's nine-stem bee balm may debut next spring with 25 stems. The following year the number may run to three figures. Fast-spreading species like bee balm will overrun less aggressive neighbors. Periodically divide such overachievers to reduce their size.

Slower-growing perennials need division, too. Unchecked growth takes a toll on a perennial's appearance and vigor. In clump-forming species, such as coral bells and daylilies, many stems growing where once there was just one means there's more competition for nutrients, water, and light. Leaves and flowers become smaller. The plant doesn't rebound as fast from problems or cutting back.

Diseases and insects thrive amid weakened tissues and find shelter in crowded stems. Pests, such as powdery mildew on garden phlox and four-lined plant bug on pincushion flower, multiply in these conditions.

The longer a perennial grows without division, the more likely it is to invite and be damaged by pests. Some perennials get into trouble quickly and should be divided every two to three years. Others can stay in place for five to six years with little or no loss in health or looks. A few need division so rarely that they can be considered permanent plants.

Some gardeners divide a plant right after it has impressed them with its mature beauty, figuring it's all downhill after the peak. Others know that a plant will gradually decline in vigor or bloom count; they wait to divide until these effects are more noticeable.

► **The character of the roots determine the type of tool to use to cut through them. Heavy shears are often enough, but cutting through the thick rhizomes of some perennials, such as solomon's seal, may require a sharp knife.**

◄ **In order to examine roots, wash away most of the soil that still clings to them. Cut away roots that are damaged.**

Choose the best season

Divide perennials in spring or fall, when plants reestablish most quickly. Cool air and warm soil result in more root than shoot growth, so transplants can really dig in. Rain is often more reliable in spring and fall and there's less evaporation, which ensures that the reduced root system can meet the plants' needs for water. Soil stays more evenly moist and thus more conducive to root growth, and there is less follow-up watering to do.

► **Because the plants are essentially bare root, replant right away. Set the divisions at the same height they grew before, or slightly higher.**

Divide spring-blooming perennials in fall and fall bloomers in spring. This provides the longest possible time for a plant to reestablish between division and its next bloom cycle. When it blooms, its roots will be more expansive, and thus, the plant will be sturdier.

Lift out plants, cut roots

Begin by digging up the mother plant and shaking off excess soil. Use a garden fork to loosen soil all around the plant. Put your fork under the plant and work the handle like a lever. Many perennials will pop right out; others will need further digging. Try to get as much root as possible, but don't hesitate to cut roots. When a perennial needs dividing most, it's not unusual to reduce its root mass and stem count by three-fourths.

Clumping plants with multiple crowns and fleshy roots, such as daylily and plantain lily, can be teased apart when young. Older plants can be more difficult to divide without cutting some of their roots. Bearded and Siberian iris have plump storage roots called rhizomes, which snap into pieces. To grow, each bit of root must have an eye (growth point) or an intact tuft of foliage. Plants such as coreopsis, with its finely netted, fibrous roots, can be gently ripped or cut into small chunks. And perennials that produce shoots from shallow runners or stems can be divided using a sharp garden knife.

Keep young plant parts

The youngest parts of a plant, usually the outside edges of a clump, are the healthiest and most vigorous. They have had the least exposure to pests, and they've received the best nutrition—from nutrients outside the main root ball in soil not yet exhausted by older plant parts.

Keep these youngest pieces. Discard the central, older parts. Clip off frayed and injured roots. Remove all weed roots that have infiltrated the perennial's root ball.

Before replanting divisions, renew the soil to replace nutrients and organic matter. Refer to page 32 for instructions.

◄ Roots of bearded iris are shallow and lift readily from the soil. Separate the new from the old rhizomes and discard the latter. Also check for rhizomes damaged by iris borer, and discard any that you find. Shorten the leaves of the healthy rhizomes and replant.

◄ Divide lamb's-ears by lifting the entire root ball and gently teasing apart the separate clumps. Trim off the leaves of each section before replanting it.

◄ Cut through the dense roots of showy sedum with a trowel, and separate clumps. Cut off old stems and leaves and replant.

PROPAGATING

Making more perennials needn't be complicated. Most are easy to propagate by division, as described on pages 44 and 45. If you want more plants and the parent plant doesn't need dividing, you can often simply slice off sections of the root in early spring. Pot up or transplant the small sections and fill in around the base of the parent with fresh soil. It will continue to grow without missing a beat.

Perennials from seed

Most perennials can be grown from seed. The process is generally the same as starting the seeds of annual flowers or vegetables.

Fill clean, freely draining small pots with moistened seed-starting soil mix. Read seed packets for instructions about planting depth or required chilling or heat. Unless the instructions advise otherwise, distribute seeds evenly on the soil mix and cover them lightly with soil mix. Keep the seeds moist and warm, about 70°F, until seedlings begin to emerge. Then move the tray or pot to a sunny window or place it on a shelf with fluorescent lights close overhead.

If instructions say the seeds require light to germinate, don't cover the seeds. Scatter them on the soil's surface, and cover the pot or tray with glass or clear plastic to maintain high humidity. Remove the cover as soon as seeds sprout.

Seed packets often list days to germination. Many perennials, such as balloon flower, shasta daisy, and basket-of-gold, germinate in about a week. Others are slower; astilbe, for example, needs almost 2 months to sprout.

Seeds of some perennials, such as butterfly weed and balloon flower, can be sown directly outdoors where you want them to grow, but you may have to nurse plants for a season or two before they flower. Late summer or fall is usually the best time to direct-sow perennials; read the label of your seed packet for specific timing.

Care for seedlings

Whether seedlings are planted indoors or out, keep them evenly moist, and make sure to provide plentiful air circulation. Adequate air circulation is important to control a seedling's worst enemy—the disease called damping-off, which causes stems to rot at the soil level. Clean pots, sterile soil mix, and good air circulation are ways to avert this problem.

▶ **Many kinds of perennials are easy to start from seed. Follow directions on the seed packet regarding timing and optimum temperatures. After germination make sure seedlings receive plenty of light. Fluorescent tubes placed about 4 inches above seedling tops provide ideal light.**

When the seedlings develop two or three true leaves, transplant them into larger pots. Feed weekly with regular fertilizer but at half strength, unless the directions specify rates for seedlings. Prevent legginess by maintaining high light intensity.

Harden seedlings gradually to the outdoors, and when their roots fill a 4-inch container, plant them in the garden. If you choose to transplant them to an intermediate-size pot, move up just one pot size at a time—from a 4-inch to a 5- or 6-inch container, and so on. Let the roots be your guide to how often to transplant: Some perennials may take two years to fill a gallon pot.

Perennials from cuttings

Growing from stem cuttings is a way to make more of perennials that don't produce a duplicate of the parent from seed, are difficult to divide, or are slow to increase to a clump size that makes division practical.

Many perennials that bloom in mid- and late summer produce stems that are well-suited for rooting by late spring or early summer. Russian sage is an example and is a good candidate for cuttings because it grows slowly and is difficult to divide. Species that bloom early in the year often produce the best stem cuttings from new shoots that develop in summer.

Choose a healthy, vigorously growing stem without flower buds to make a cutting. Make sure that it is firm and not too soft and flexible (if it bends without snapping, it's too soft). Snip a 4- to 6-inch section of this stem, remove its lower leaves, and stick it, cut side down, into moist potting mix, coarse sand, or perlite. Push it deeply enough into the soil to bury the nodes or joints stripped bare of leaves.

Some perennial species root best from tip cuttings. Others, such as bleeding heart and stoke's aster, have tips that are never quite firm enough, so you will need to discard the tip and use a cutting from nearer the base of the stem.

Protect cuttings from drying out during the time it takes them to form roots. Keep the soil moist, but never wet enough to encourage rot. Grow them where they are shaded from the midday sun. Most cuttings root within a month.

Transplant rooted cuttings into the garden as you would any other potted plant once their roots have filled their pots and they have been hardened.

◄ With soil and pots ready to receive them, prepare cuttings by removing lower leaves.

▶ Use your finger or a pencil to make a narrow hole, and place the cuttings in pots.

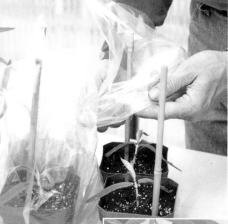

◄ To maintain high humidity around the leaves, cover pots with plastic bags. Use narrow bamboo stakes or coat hangers to support the plastic and keep it from touching the leaves.

▶ After about a month and once you can see evidence of new growth, gently slip a root ball out of a pot to check root growth. When you see that the roots are well developed, you can plant in the garden.

WEEDS AND WEEDING

The best way to manage weeds in a perennial garden is by eliminating them before you plant. At that point, without plants to work around, ridding the soil of weeds is much simpler. After planting, mulch will suppress most weeds, leaving only the occasional interloper to pluck here or there. But often you don't have the option of starting with a clean slate.

There are two basic kinds of weeds; knowing the difference between them will help you cope with each one. Some, such as dandelions, are clumpers, and others, such as ground ivy, are runners.

▶ For weeds with running rhizomes such as quackgrass, remove as much of the rhizome as possible to limit regrowth.

▼ To eliminate a dandelion, remove the entire taproot; otherwise sections that remain will make new plants.

■ **Runners** keep moving by sending their creeping roots or stems into new areas and making new roots and plants. Ground ivy and bindweed are examples. Loosen the soil where you see sprouts of these plants and pull gently, beginning at the center of the colony and working out to the newest shoots. This may be the only way to find and remove runners that have not yet sent shoots to the surface.

Preventing weeds

After a thorough weeding, suppress new weeds by applying a 2-inch layer of mulch. The mulch denies weed seeds the light that many need to germinate. Those that do manage to germinate and grow exhaust their energy reserves growing through the layer to reach light and are easy to pull. If weed problems are severe, you can supplement the mulch by first spreading a preemergence herbicide, such as corn gluten meal, and then mulching.

■ **Clumpers**, such as burdock, dandelion, and Canada thistle, are able to regrow even after all top growth is removed; therefore, you must remove as much of the root as possible. Use a dandelion digger, garden fork, trowel, or knife to loosen the soil around the weed, then pull. Always mulch an area bared by weed removal; that bare soil is likely to be full of seeds the removed plant has left behind.

▶ After weeding an area, cover it with mulch. Mulch will prevent dormant weed seeds from sprouting and taking the place of the weeds you just removed.

PESTS

▲ **A forceful spray of water knocks most aphids off tender shoots.**

The pests that trouble perennials are as diverse as the plants themselves. Among them are insects such as aphids and caterpillars, snails, slugs, Japanese beetles, and animals such as rabbits, deer, and woodchucks.

Routinely patrolling your garden for problems is the first step in making a diagnosis and is key to keeping pests from getting out of control. Once you discover a problem, it's important to properly identify its cause. Only then can you select the appropriate solution.

Most of the insects and other critters that live in our gardens are harmless. Only a few are either beneficial or harmful. Learn about the common pests that cause problems in your area, watch for them, and don't let the others alarm you. For more information, check with your county extension service.

Controlling insects, snails, and slugs

▓ **Aphids** are pear-shaped, soft-bodied, winged or wingless insects about ⅛-inch long. They cluster on the softest growing tips of stems early in the season and often cause distorted growth.
Control: Many other insects prey on aphids, which helps reduce their numbers. Also, infestations in spring usually fade away with the first heat of summer. In the meantime, knock aphids off with a strong spray of water, insecticidal soap, or other insecticide labeled for aphid control such

▲ **If you see curling, distorted leaves on your perennials in spring, check with a hand lens. You'll likely see tiny aphids.**

▼ **One of the most vexing pests of perennials is the iris borer. Watch for stained, water-soaked leaves in spring. also look for holes bored into leaves.**

as Ortho Bug-B-Gon MAX Lawn & Garden Insect Killer.

▓ **Iris borers and other caterpillars** are the larvae of moths and butterflies. In the fall, iris borers lay eggs in old leaf and flower stalks; they hatch the following spring. At first the larvae feed on the surface of leaves, but eventually they bore their way inside of tissue and down to the rhizome. The typical symptom is dark, water-soaked streaks in new leaves. Other caterpillars, such as the white cabbage butterfly, fruitworm, and tent caterpillar, feed on the leaves of many kinds of perennials.
Control: Clean up and destroy plant debris in early spring to reduce iris borer problems. Squeeze leaves in the vicinity of feeding damage to kill feeding borers inside. Use beneficial nematodes *(Steinernema carpocapsae)* to reduce severe infestations. Protect perennials susceptible to other caterpillar damage by covering them with a floating row cover. Also, you can kill young caterpillars with the biological control Bt *(Bacillus thuringiensis)*, which is harmless to people, animals, and beneficial insects. Spray with insecticide as necessary, making sure the label lists the insect you plan to target.

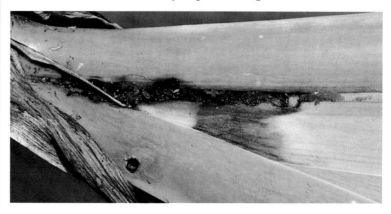

Japanese beetles are ½-inch-long metallic blue or green beetles with coppery wings. The adults consume leaves and flowers, leaving only skeletons of leaf veins. The grubs overwinter in the soil and eat grass roots in spring.
Control: Start by handpicking adult beetles and dropping or knocking them off plants into soapy water. To reduce the number of grubs, apply either milky spore disease, beneficial nematodes, or both to lawns in early spring. Reduce adult feeding damage by spraying with Ortho Systemic Insect Killer Concentrate.

Columbine leaf miners produce distinctive white or gray winding trails in the leaves of columbine. Small adult flies make tiny pinholes in leaves in which they deposit their eggs.
Control: Remove and destroy all plant remains in the fall, and pick off damaged leaves during the growing season. Botanical insecticides such as neem are effective controls if applied early. To rescue plants from severe infestations, use Ortho Systemic Insect Killer Concentrate, permethrin, resmethrin, or imidacloprid.
Earwigs are ½-inch-long brown insects with pincers at the rear of their bodies. During the day they hide in crevices and under garden debris. At night, the nymphs or immature insects chew holes in leaves, stems, flowers, and fruit.
Control: Trap earwigs by laying pieces of folded-up newspaper on the soil overnight; in the morning, collect and dispose of papers and all the earwigs that have taken refuge inside them. If earwigs persist, spray with Ortho Bug-Geta Plus Snail, Slug & Insect Killer.

▲ **Meandering trails inside columbine leaves are made by the feeding of tiny leaf miner larvae.**

▶ **Japanese beetles can do a lot of damage, but they're easy to pick off leaves.**

▲ **Slugs feeding make large holes in leaves.**

◀ **Earwigs prefer to nibble on succulent flower petals.**

Slugs and snails are moisture-loving creatures that rasp large holes in leaves and flower petals.
Control: Discourage them by removing garden debris. Hunt for them in the evening, using a flashlight to spot them. Set shallow saucers of beer under plants to lure and drown them. Or, use snail baits such as Ortho Bug-Geta Plus Snail, Slug & Insect Killer. Baits containing iron phosphate are not toxic to birds and bees.

Animal pests

Furry and feathered friends sometimes are hard on gardens. Here's how to cope.

■ **Birds** occasionally damage plants by feeding on or uprooting seedlings or injuring foliage in pursuit of pests.
Control: Protect young or special plants. Cover plants with bird netting or a row cover, or set up scarecrows.

■ **Deer** prefer but do not limit their feeding to young growth and flower buds. In winter, they may paw up and feed on the crowns of perennial plants.
Control: Install electric fencing or barriers at least 8 feet tall for deer. Dark plastic mesh fencing is effective and reasonably priced. Set up motion-sensitive scarecrows. These startle intruders with water sprays or sound and are effective from spring to fall if kept in the same location. Some plants are deer-resistant, but if deer are hungry enough they'll eat almost anything.

▲ **Excluding deer with a fence is the only sure way to prevent their feeding.**

▶ **Rabbits often work from the bottom toward the top of a plant and may prefer the side of a plant or garden that is closer to shelter.**

◀ **Groundhogs find perennial flowers to be a tasty treat. Protect your garden with fencing or by live-trapping of problem animals.**

■ **Groundhogs, pocket gophers, and prairie dogs** are all powerful diggers. Groundhogs (or woodchucks) can climb pretty well too, if it means getting at their preferred fresh flower buds. Prairie dogs eat mostly grass but also flowers, roots, and insects. Gophers eat roots of just about anything.
Control: Protect individual plants or gardens from groundhogs with chicken wire or fencing. Because these animals dig so well, an underground section of fencing is just as important. Bury it 12 inches deep, with an 8-inch L bottom section that extends away from the garden. Pocket gophers are best managed by using traps placed in main tunnels.

Both groundhogs and prairie dogs are relatively easy to live-trap, but local ordinances often limit relocation. Check with local animal control officials.

■ **Rabbits** nibble foliage and neatly snip off individual stems and leaves of many perennials. Damage is often heaviest early in the year.
Control: Protect small plants by surrounding them with chicken wire. It may make more sense to surround the entire garden area with an 18- to 24-inch-high fence. Where rabbits are numerous, they may try digging under the fence. In that case, bend the wire to make an 8-inch L at the bottom of the fence, facing out. Then bury the L under mulch. Some gardeners find motion-activated electronic devices that startle rabbits with water sprays or sound to be effective. Repellants can be effective, but they require repeated applications.

PERENNIALS SELECTION GUIDE

This section features more than 200 of the finest perennials that are available today. You'll learn about each plant's preferred growing conditions, how to place it for best effect, special needs, and tips for day-to-day care.

Key to the entries

Each of the plants is described in the following ways:

■ **Scientific name:** The universally accepted Latin name is comprised of first the genus name followed by a species name and is shown in italics. It's comparable to your own name, only in reverse, with a surname followed by your given name, as in Smith Kathy. Hybrid plants are indicated by a multiplication sign between the genus and species name. An example of a hybrid is *Calamagrostis ×acutiflora*.

▼ **Perennials including beebalm, garden phlox, and daylily combine to produce a gloriously colorful border.**

Often there's another name following the genus and species. Called the cultivar, it's the name of a plant that's propagated asexually, such as by division or cuttings. This name is not italicized but is capitalized and separated by single quotation marks. A Latin name with a cultivar is written this way: *Calamagrostis ×acutiflora* 'Karl Foerster'.

Because botanical science evolves (and sometimes botanists disagree), discrepancies in Latin names occur. For this book, our reference has been the *List of Names of Perennials* (5th edition, by M.H.A. Hoffman, Applied Plant Research, The Netherlands, 2005). The book is available from the Perennial Plant Association at www.perennialplant.org.

■ **Common name:** This is the everyday name of a plant, but be aware that many plants have several common names. In the example above, the common name is 'Karl Foerster' feather reed grass. In practice it's not unusual to need both Latin and common names to confirm the identity of a plant.

■ **Key features:** Bullet points designate each plant's cold and heat hardiness zones, preferred exposure, size, and significant ornamental features.

Hardiness zone ratings are the most available and convenient way to determine whether a given plant will survive in your garden. Based on weather data, the USDA Plant Hardiness Zone Map (page 122) shows where plants are likely to survive the rigors of winter. While hardiness based on winter cold is the single most useful guide to plant hardiness, it is only one. Snow cover, wind, humidity, and summer heat all play significant roles in plant hardiness.

Because summer high temperatures are as limiting to some plants as winter lows are to others, the American Horticultural Society developed the Plant Heat Zone Map. It divides the continental United States into 12 zones from the coolest Zone 1, which averages only one day per season hotter than 86°F, to the hottest Zone 12, which averages 210 days warmer than 86°F.

"Light" notes the degree of exposure to sunlight the plant requires, and "size" is the average mature size. Keep in mind that soil and climate will have a significant effect on mature size.

The text that follows the bulleted list is a more specific description of the plant and any specialized maintenance it needs aside from standard care. And, finally, there's mention of outstanding cultivars and related species that are available.

PLANT GALLERY

Acanthus spinosus
Spiny bear's breeches

- Hardiness Zones: 5–10
- Heat Zones: 12–1
- Light: Full to half sun
- Size: 3–4'H×3'W
- Features: White flowers with dusky maroon bracts, late spring (South) or early summer (North)

Spiny bear's breeches

Spiny bear's breeches feature sturdy 4-foot spires of white flowers and huge, dark, glossy leaves are spined but not sharp. Plant this big grower in the middle or front of a border if there's space to accommodate it.

Slow growing at first, it picks up speed and may form a large colony. In warm regions, spiny bear's breeches is heat and drought tolerant as well as evergreen. **Care:** In warmer areas, provide some shade during the heat of the day; it may bloom less than in cooler regions. Spiny bear's breeches is generally pest free, but slugs and snails may be a problem.

Obtain new plants by digging near the crown in spring. Cut off several inches of the pencil-thin roots and plant the cut end up. Flowering stalks can be attractive after bloom.

Achillea
Yarrow

- Hardiness Zones: 3–9
- Heat Zones: 9–2
- Light: Full sun
- Size: 18–60"H×18–36"W
- Features: Yellow, white, red, or pink flowers depending on species, late spring to midsummer

Yarrow has fernlike foliage and distinctive flat-topped flower clusters. Some species are mounded in leaf, columnar in bloom; others form mats. Eighteen- to 24-inch varieties are as tall as wide. Plants tolerate drought and dry soil.
Care: Cut stems to the ground after the bloom season ends to encourage new basal foliage. Yarrow is mostly pest-free; rabbits and deer find it unpalatable.
Recommended plants and related species: Common yarrow (*A. millefolium*) is a low-growing, rapidly spreading perennial. 'Appleblossom' has peach to lilac-pink flowers and is 2 to 3 feet tall. 'Paprika' flowers are an intense red with yellow centers on 2-foot stems. Fern-leaf yarrow (*A. filipendulina*) reaches 3 to 5 feet in bloom. The hybrid 'Coronation Gold' is one of the best for drying. Another hybrid, 'Moonshine', has brilliant yellow flowers and 1-foot-tall silvery foliage that is covered with soft hairs.

Common yarrow

Aconitum carmichaelii
Azure monkshood

- Hardiness Zones: 3–8
- Heat Zones: 8–3
- Light: Full sun to partial shade
- Size: 2–4'H×1'W
- Features: Blue flowers, late summer or fall

Azure monkshood

Azure monkshood is an upright, clump-forming perennial and is a good companion for goatsbeard and Kamchatka bugbane. All parts of monkshood plants are poisonous.
Care: Keep soil continuously moist. Azure monkshood does not do well in heat or where nighttime temperatures are above 70°F; midday shade may be necessary. Fertilize more than average. Wilting in early spring is a sign of crown rot; remedy by improving winter drainage. Azure monkshood resists rabbits and deer. Deadheading prolongs bloom in areas with extended autumn. Cut back to the ground in late fall. Remove and destroy prunings to prevent disease.
Recommended plants and related species: 'Arendsii' has large blue flowers in fall. Bicolor monkshood (*A. × cammarum* 'Bicolor') has white hoods with a blue border and grows 3 to 4 feet tall in Zones 3 to 7. *A. septentrionale* 'Ivorine', the earliest to flower, has creamy white flowers on compact plants and grows 2 to 3 feet tall.

Acorus calamus
Sweet flag

- Hardiness Zones: 4–8
- Heat Zones: 12–2
- Light: Full sun to partial shade
- Size: 2–3'H×2'W
- Features: Attractive, grassy leaves that are fragrant when crushed

Variegated sweet flag

Sweet flag earned its name for the unique lemony fragrance in its leaves and roots. While at first glance it appears related to the grasses or iris family perhaps, it's actually more similar to calla lily. Greenish flowers come on a 2- to 3-inch, callalike stalk.

Sweet flag grows throughout North America, usually in or near shallow water next to lakes or rivers. Plants make excellent bog or aquatic specimens, and do well near swimming pools.
Care: Plants tolerate soggy soil but will thrive in soils that are merely well-watered.
Recommended plants and related species: *A. calamus* 'Variegatus' is the most popular form and bears long, narrow leaves with well-defined creamy white bands. *A. americanus* is native throughout North America. *A. gramineus,* dwarf sweet flag, grows to only 1 foot tall.

Actaea simplex
(Cimicifuga simplex)
Kamchatka bugbane

- Hardiness Zones: 4–7
- Heat Zones: 10–1
- Light: Half to full shade
- Size: 3–5'H×2'W
- Features: White flowers, late summer into fall

Kamchatka bugbane is studded with white buds that tease from July until mid- to late fall, finally opening to ivory bottlebrushes after first frost. Good companions include jacob's ladder, brunnera, and lungwort. All plant parts are toxic, but the highest concentration of toxins is in the berries and root. Plants form clumps or spread slowly by rhizomes.
Care: Best growth occurs in soils that are continuously moist or regularly watered. There are no special fertilizer needs, and the plant is pest-free. Cut it to the ground in late fall after frost kills the top. For more plants, sow fresh seed directly outdoors in early fall after soaking berries to remove pulp from seed. The plant needs several weeks of 70°F temperatures, then several months at or below 40°F and a gradual warm-up in spring for complete germination.
Recommended plants and related species: 'Prichard's Giant' grows 4 to 5 feet tall. Leaves and stems of 'Brunette' are purplish.

Kamchatka bugbane

Adiantum pedatum
Maidenhair fern

- Hardiness Zones: 3–8
- Heat Zones: 9–3
- Light: Half to full shade
- Size: 10–24"H×18"W
- Features: Delicate and lacy; light green fronds

Maidenhair fern

One of the most beautiful and refined ferns, maidenhair has fronds with an unusual five-finger pattern on shiny black stems. This elegant fern is gorgeous in moist woodland gardens and as a filler in bouquets. It looks magnificent when paired with solomon's seal or hosta.
Care: Grow ferns 18 inches apart in filtered light and continuously moist soil. Add agricultural lime to acid soils according to soil test results. Keep soil moist during dry summer months.
Recommended plants and related species: 'Japonicum' fronds emerge pinkish bronze. 'Miss Sharples' has chartreuse new growth and larger leaflets. Evergreen maidenhair (*A. venustum*) grows 12 inches tall with pale green fronds on purplish black stems. Fronds have a blue tint in summer and turn yellow-brown in autumn. Southern maidenhair fern (*A. capillus-veneris*) glistens in shade (Zones 7 to 10).

Agastache foeniculum
Anise hyssop

- **Hardiness Zones: 5–10**
- **Heat Zones: 12–5**
- **Light: Full sun to partial shade**
- **Size: 2–4'H×2–3'W**
- **Features: Dense spikes of purple flowers, midsummer to autumn**

Anise hyssop with stonecrop

Anise hyssop is an upright, licorice-scented perennial. This plant spreads, increasing in size at a moderate to fast pace. It complements the shape and texture of Chinese peony, black-eyed susan, garden phlox, and meadow rue. And it blooms at the same time as late-season daylilies, bee balm, and purple coneflower. **Care:** Grow in well-drained, slightly alkaline soil. The plant requires no special fertilizer treatments and has few pest or disease problems. Cut back plants to the ground in late fall. Anise hyssop reseeds readily. It is rabbit- and deer-resistant.
Recommended plants and related species: 'Blue Fortune' grows to 4 feet (or more) tall and 2 feet wide. Its blue-purple blooms last from June until September. 'Firebird' has interesting salmon to pink flowers; it may be hardy only to Zone 6.

Alcea rosea
Hollyhock

- **Hardiness Zones: 3–7**
- **Heat Zones: 10–3**
- **Light: Full sun**
- **Size: 4–8'H×2'W**
- **Features: Towering flower spikes, early to midsummer**

Short-lived and often considered a biennial, hollyhock is a must for the cottage garden and back of the border. Great for a vertical effect or even a living screen, the plant is prized for its old-fashioned charm. Combine hollyhock with old-fashioned, daisylike sun lovers, such as helenium, black-eyed susan, or purple coneflower. **Care:** Hollyhock grows easily from seed and thrives in rich, well-drained soil. Space transplants or seeds 12 inches apart. The plant is vulnerable to slugs, leaf miners, Japanese beetles, and hollyhock rust. Remove diseased foliage as soon as it appears. Select newer cultivars, which are less rust-susceptible. Although short-lived, hollyhock self-sows, ensuring its continued presence.
Recommended plants and related species: Chater's Double Group has double flowers in maroon, red, rose, white, or yellow. 'Nigra' is a single; it is called black hollyhock because of its wine-purple blooms. Double-flowered 'Peaches 'n' Dreams' blooms the first year from seeds, and grows to 7 feet tall.

'Peaches 'n' Dreams' hollyhock

Alchemilla mollis
Lady's mantle

- **Hardiness Zones: 3–7**
- **Heat Zones: 9–1**
- **Light: Half sun to shade**
- **Size: 1'H×2–3'W**
- **Features: Airy sprays of yellow-green flowers, late spring to early summer**

Lady's mantle

Tiny chartreuse flowers arch from foot-tall mounds of marvelous gray-green leaves. The downy foliage is a main attraction, with each leaf emerging like pleated velvet and fanning into a circle. Flower stems hover 3 to 6 inches above the leaves. The growth rate is moderate. Its foliage combines well with fringed bleeding heart and Japanese toad lily. It blooms at the same time as bellflower and oriental poppy. **Care:** Grow in well-drained, moist soil; there are no special fertilizer needs. Strip off old foliage in early spring, but avoid cutting plants back hard, because new growth buds form above ground on the semiwoody crown. You can mow to clean up plants in spring; set the mower at 4 inches. Lady's mantle rarely needs division. Deadhead to prevent reseeding.
Recommended plants and related species: Alpine lady's mantle (*A. alpina*) is only 6 inches tall. The underside of each deeply lobed leaf has fine hairs, which create a silky, silvery outline.

Amsonia tabernaemontana
Blue star

- Hardiness Zones: 3–9
- Heat Zones: 8–4
- Light: Partial shade or full sun
- Size: 2–4'H×3'W
- Features: Clusters of blue starlike flowers, spring

Blue star

Resembling a shrubby willow tree, North American native blue star is long lived and low maintenance. Effective in masses, it has a soft texture that contrasts with other garden plants. Rarely invasive, it grows slowly and pairs beautifully with bergenia or cushion spurge, and it makes a lovely companion for peonies. **Care:** Set nursery plants 12 inches apart. Division is seldom necessary; pests and diseases are not a problem. Shear after flowering, no more than one-third to one-half, so that plants won't grow too tall. The plant's milky sap may cause burning or itching.
Recommended plants and related species: Arkansas amsonia *(A. hubrictii)* has lacy foliage, steel- blue flowers, and brilliant yellow fall foliage color. It is one of the best perennials for reliable autumn color.

Anaphalis triplinervis
Three-veined everlasting

- Hardiness Zones: 3–8
- Heat Zones: 8–3
- Light: Full to half sun
- Size: 12–18"H×1–2'W
- Features: White blooms, midsummer to late summer

Clusters of white pearls on this mounded-shape plant open to yellow-centered buttons with crisp petals. A spreading perennial, three-veined everlasting grows fast. Combine it with bear's breeches, speedwell, threadleaf coreopsis, and 'Husker Red' penstemon for a colorful display. **Care:** Grow in well-drained, preferably moist soil. Fertilize only modestly to avoid rank, weak growth. Clean up plants in early spring, and divide them every four to five years.

Three-veined everlasting is an occasional larval host of the American painted lady butterfly. Tolerate caterpillars on established plants; they finish feeding in time for plants to recover and bloom. Plants are deer and rabbit resistant.
Recommended plants and related species: 'Summer Snow' is a dwarf that is good for edging. Pearly everlasting *(A. margaritacea)* is more drought tolerant but less tolerant of heavy or wet soils. It's taller, to 36 inches, later-blooming by two weeks, and less likely to need staking. Japanese pearly everlasting *(A. margaritacea* var. *yedoensis)* has larger flowers than the species and, with snow cover, is hardy to Zone 3.

Three-veined everlasting

Anemone × hybrida
Hybrid anemone, Japanese anemone

- Hardiness Zones: 5–8
- Heat Zones: 9–3
- Light: Full sun to shade
- Size: 2–5'H×1–2'W
- Features: White, pink, or mauve flowers, late summer to fall

Hybrid anemone

For most of the summer, plants of hybrid anemone hug the ground. Anemones bear clusters of flowers on stems that in bloom reach 3 feet tall. The silky sheen of the 2- to 3-inch blossoms perks up late-summer gardens for weeks. **Care:** Plant in moist, well-drained soil. Avoid sites that are hot or have strong winds, wet soil, or drought. Anemones spread by rhizomes and can form large, dense colonies. Plants rarely set viable seed. Cut them back in late fall. Heavy mulch or reliable snow cover increases hardiness to Zone 4. Plants are rabbit resistant.
Recommended plants and related species: 'Honorine Jobert' has white single flowers, grows 3 to 4 feet tall, and is sun- and drought-tolerant. Flowers are smaller than those on other varieties. 'Queen Charlotte' has semidouble pale mauve flowers, and grows 3 feet tall. 'Whirlwind' has semidouble large white flowers and grows 3 to 5 feet. *A. hupehensis* 'September Charm' has single pink flowers.

Anthemis tinctoria
Golden marguerite

- **Hardiness Zones: 3–7**
- **Heat Zones: 8–3**
- **Light: Full to half sun**
- **Size: 2–3'H×2'W**
- **Features: Yellow or white daisies, early to midsummer**

Golden marguerite

These plants have masses of bright yellow daisies, and are fast-growing. They spread by ground-level offsets and seed. The fragrant, finely divided, deep green foliage and upright habit combine well with brunnera, daylily, and fountain grass.
Care: Grow golden marguerite in well-drained soil. The plant tolerates drought and heat. Deadhead to prolong bloom and prevent seed set. Cut plants back after the bloom fades to promote new basal growth. Apply fertilizer at half the average rate to avoid soft, floppy growth. Stake with crutches or grow-through supports. The plant is easy to grow from seed or division. Divide plants every two to three years before the oldest, central portion of the clump dies out; offsets are easy to move.
Recommended plants and related species: 'Moonlight', 2 feet tall, has pale yellow flowers. 'Kelwayi', which grows 3 feet tall, has more finely cut foliage and brighter yellow flowers. 'E.C. Buxton' has creamy yellow flowers and finely cut foliage.

Aquilegia
Columbine

- **Hardiness Zones: 3–9**
- **Heat Zones: 9–3**
- **Light: Half to full sun; midday shade prolongs bloom period**
- **Size: 1–3'H×1'W**
- **Features: Yellow, salmon, red, blue, or white midspring blooms**

Columbine's nicely textured foliage is topped by sturdy, upright, branched flower stalks, which double or triple the height of the plant. Blooms may be single- or multicolored. Clump-forming plants grow fast, and the flowers attract hummingbirds. Combine columbine with foam flower and woodland phlox or hydrangeas. The foliage is a good foil for toad lily.
Care: Grow in well-drained soil, and fertilize generously. Deadhead to prolong bloom. As flower buds swell, check leaves for leaf-miner damage (see page 50). Clean up dead foliage in late fall. Plants are relatively short-lived, and dividing is usually not necessary. They will self-sow. Red-flowered types with hanging blooms generally require wetter soil and are less tolerant of drought.

Recommended plants and related species: Blue-flowered columbines descend from the Rocky Mountain columbine (*A. caerulea*), and prefer more sun and cooler summers. They also tolerate drier soil. The McKana Hybrids are noted for extra-long flower spurs and a wide variety of colors. They grow

Rocky Mountain columbine

to 2 feet tall. Species columbine, particularly the bicolored red and yellow Canadian columbine (*A. canadensis*), may be more resistant to leaf miners.

McKana Hybrid columbine

Arabis caucasica
Wall rock cress

- Hardiness Zones: 4–7
- Heat Zones: 8–1
- Light: Half to full sun
- Size: 8–12"H×18"W
- Features: White flowers, early spring

Wall rock cress

This mat-forming, grayish evergreen spreads by rooting where its stems contact moist soil. It forms colonies at a moderate to fast rate—a well-sited 6-inch-wide plant may be 18 inches wide at the end of a season. Wall rock cress, which can be used as a groundcover, is attractive with columbine, masterwort, and lungwort. Or pair it with other evergreen perennials.

Care: Plant in well-drained and neutral or slightly alkaline soil. Fertilize at half typical rates. Rather than cut the evergreen plants back in fall, trim after bloom by shearing. If necessary, divide after flowering. Powdery mildew, rust, and aphids sometimes pose problems, as does club root. Look for deformed, shortened roots on plants that fail to thrive or decline. Destroy infected plants. Avoid planting other members of the mustard family where club root has been a problem.

Recommended plants and related species: 'Flore Pleno' has double flowers, is later to bloom than the species, and tends to stay in bloom longer.

Arisaema
Jack-in-the-pulpit

- Hardiness Zones: 4–9
- Heat Zones: 9–1
- Light: Shade
- Size: 12–30"H×24"W
- Features: Exotic flowers in spring, bright berries in fall

This native relative of calla lily is outstanding naturalized in woodland gardens. Plants grow from tubers that produce one to three leaves in spring. Each leaf is divided into three or more leaflets. Tiny flowers come on a club-shape spike, called a spadix, that is surrounded by a green or purplish leaf, called a spathe. Flowers mature into bright orange or red berries.

Care: Plant in cool and moist soil that is rich in organic matter. Plant knobby tubers in fall, 1 foot apart, 2 to 4 inches deep, and then leave them alone. Plants die to ground in winter. Trap or bait snails and slugs.

Recommended plants and related species: With more than 150 species from all over the world, there are many to choose from. The club-shape, white flowers of gaudy jack, *A. sikokianum,* are followed by red berries. Jack-in-the-pulpit, *A. triphyllum,* produces two leaves that have three lobes each. The color of the drooping spathe varies between purple with green to solid green. Berries are bright red.

Gaudy jack

Armeria maritima
Thrift

- Hardiness Zones: 4–8
- Heat Zones: 9–4
- Light: Full sun; partial shade in hot areas
- Size: 6"H×6–12"W
- Features: Pink or creamy white flowers, midspring

Thrift

Lollipop clusters of blooms top evergreen, grassy tufts that resemble clean deep-green cushions. Flower stalks double the height of this clump-forming plant; its growth rate is moderate. Thrift complements the gray-green foliage of cupid's dart and the swordlike spears of iris. It blooms with catmint.

Care: Plant in well-drained soil, ideally sandy and with a neutral to alkaline pH. Deadhead to keep young plants blooming through the summer; older clumps will rebloom sporadically. Avoid cutting plants back in fall. If the center dies, dig it out and transplant from the margins. Propagate by division, cuttings, or seed. Cuttings root readily, and seeds germinate easily.

Recommended plants and related species: 'Ruby Glow' flowers are nearly red. Those of 'Düsseldorf Pride' are deep rose, but the plant is less cold-hardy than the species. Pyrenees thrift, *A. juniperifolia* 'Bevan's Variety', is a 4-inch dwarf with pink, nearly stemless flowers.

Artemisia
Artemisia

- **Hardiness Zones: 4–9**
- **Heat Zones: 8–4**
- **Light: Full sun**
- **Size: 6–72"H×12–48"W**
- **Features: Silvery gray-green foliage**

White sage with yarrow

Most artemisias have magnificent silvery pubescent foliage that complements a range of other plants in the perennial garden. Their inconspicuous whitish flowers appear in late summer. For the most part, artemisias are well-behaved, although some, like white sage, spread aggressively. Use spreading forms only where you can control their growth. Artemisias make a fine backdrop for blue and purple flowers, such as speedwell, Rocky Mountain columbine, and meadow sage, and other plants with purple foliage. The subtle colors of artemisias' foliage tone down flowers that are a strong red or orange.

Care: Plant in well-drained, neutral to slightly alkaline soil. Apply fertilizer at half the average rate. Artemisias may need staking in rich soils; use a grow-through stake. Plants that fall over can be sheared back by one-third to one-half. Deadheading is not necessary, spent flowers are not conspicuous, and self-sowing is not a problem. Divide plants every three years, discarding the oldest, central portion. Reduce plant spread as desired in spring. Stem cuttings taken in midsummer root readily. Seed requires dry, warm storage for several months before it will germinate. Avoid cutting plants back in fall. Because they are woody perennials, wait until spring, then prune off any dead stems. Stem and root rots can be a problem if the summer is hot and humid or drainage poor. Painted lady butterfly caterpillars may feed on artemisias. Leaf rust sometimes occurs. Plants are deer- and rabbit-resistant. Where artemisias have become weedy, dig out the invasive roots to control them.

Recommended plants and related species: Silvery 'Lambrook Silver' wormwood, *A. absinthium,* has filigreed leaves and grows up to 2½ feet tall.

'Powis Castle', a hybrid, is finely textured, 3 to 4 feet tall, and hardy to Zone 6.

'Guizho' white mugwort *(A. lactiflora)* found in Zones 3 to 8 (Heat Zones 12 to 8), differs from the rest by having dark green foliage. Long-lasting sprays of white flowers rise 4 to 6 feet over a low mound of leaves. Plants are slow to recover when moved.

Silver mound artemisia

White sage *(A. ludoviciana)* is often confused with dusty miller, but its crushed leaves have a distinct scent. Taller than wide (2 to 3 feet × 2 feet), the plant gives the overall impression of vertical lines. It spreads by shallow rhizomes and grows very fast.

'Powis Castle' artemisia

'Silver King', a white sage cultivar, is 3 feet tall and deep silver, and 'Silver Queen', which is 2½ feet tall and silver-gray with jagged leaf edges, are almost identical and can be mislabeled. Both are aggressive spreaders. 'Valerie Finnis', grows 18 inches tall and is less aggressive.

Silver mound artemisia *(A. schmidtiana)* is a 1-to 2-foot mound of silky, finely cut foliage. It performs best in cool areas and in soil that is not too fertile. Where it's hot and humid the center flops opens by midsummer. Beach wormwood *(A. stelleriana)* tolerates salt spray and water. The foliage is exceptionally furry and more coarsely textured than that of other artemisias. It grows 1 to 2 feet tall and 2 to 3 feet wide in Zones 3 to 8. 'Silver Brocade' is an excellent, low-growing specimen, only 6 to 8 inches tall. It is less adapted to the hot, humid Southeast region but does well in containers there.

Aruncus dioicus
Goatsbeard

- **Hardiness Zones: 3–7**
- **Heat Zones: 10–1**
- **Light: Partial to dense shade**
- **Size: 4–6'H×3–6'W**
- **Features: Off-white plumes, late spring to early summer**

Goatsbeard

This perennial and its airy off-white plumes could be mistaken for a small shrub. Its growth rate is slow to moderate. Combine this upright, medium-textured plant with mounded perennials such as geranium or bleeding heart. Play its light green foliage off of darker green turtlehead or blue-green hostas.
Care: The plant is basically pest free. Leaf spot, rust, or leaf scorch may develop, usually where the site is too dry or hot. It resists deer and rabbit damage. The dense root system requires a saw for dividing, though division is rarely needed. Goatsbeard may self-sow but not to a troublesome degree.

Do not deadhead until you see whether you like the seedheads, which can provide winter interest.
Recommended plants and related species: The cultivar 'Kneiffii' is 3 feet tall in bloom (half of which is flower stalk). Its foliage is finely cut and lacy. Dwarf goatsbeard (*A. aethusifolius*) is just 12 inches tall in bloom, a mound of finely cut foliage and dainty white spike flowers. In bloom two weeks earlier than the species, dwarf goatsbeard is a good edging plant.

Asarum
Wild ginger

- **Hardiness Zones: 3–9**
- **Heat Zones: 9–3**
- **Light: Partial to full shade**
- **Size: 6–8"H×12"W**
- **Features: Rich green, heart-shape leaves that hug ground**

Wild gingers are attractive perennials that spread via rhizomes to form a lush carpet of green. Crushed roots smell like culinary ginger, but that's as far as the similarity goes. Particularly useful as small-area groundcovers in shaded areas, wild gingers produce brownish-red, bell-shape flowers hidden by foliage.
Care: Wild gingers are adaptable but prefer and spread best in woodland soil that is rich with leaf litter and humus. They need soil that is moist but never soggy. Set plants about a foot apart; watch for slugs and snails.
Recommended plants and related species: The best is European wild ginger, *A. europaeum*. It is more generally robust than most wild gingers so serves particularly well as a ground cover. Shuttleworth ginger, *A. shuttleworthii*, is native to the Southeast and more tolerant of heat; look for variegated 'Callaway Green'. Canadian wild ginger, *A. canadense*, has leaves about 6 inches wide and is better for Zones 3 and 4. Leaves of British Columbia wild ginger, *A. caudatum*, are rounded; the flowers have long tails.

Canadian wild ginger

Asclepias tuberosa
Butterfly weed

- **Hardiness Zones: 4–9**
- **Heat Zones: 10–2**
- **Light: Full sun**
- **Size: 2–3'H×2'W**
- **Features: Bright orange or yellow flowers, midsummer**

Butterfly weed

A native prairie plant, butterfly weed is loved primarily for its colorful, vibrant blooms. Because butterflies have a special affinity with the plant, it is a must for butterfly gardens. The bright orange flowers appear as flaring clusters of ¼-inch-diameter individual flowers. This coarse-texture, vase-shape perennial is sturdy, clump forming, long lived, and slow growing.
Care: Plant in any well-drained soil. Deadheading promotes rebloom several weeks later. Cut plants back in late fall. Propagate established plants by division. Heat is necessary for plants to prosper and bloom well. When stressed they may suffer from aphid infestation; if so, check drainage. Monarch butterfly larvae feed on this plant, so you may notice some leaf damage.
Recommended plants and related species: Gay Butterflies Group is a seed mixture that offers orange, yellow, and red flowers on 2- to 3-feet-tall plants. 'High Yellow' has bright yellow flowers. For moist soils, plant swamp milkweed (*A. incarnata*). It has fragrant mauve flowers.

Aster
Aster

- **Hardiness Zones: 4–8**
- **Heat Zones: 9–1**
- **Light: Full to half sun**
- **Size: 18–60"H×18–36"W**
- **Features: Flowers of white, violet, pink, or near blue, late summer and fall**

New England aster

Asters are among the most outstanding fall-blooming perennials. Because some are common along roadsides and in fields in the East, they are easily taken for granted. But avoid those thoughts. There are many aster species and cultivars, but most produce flowers in clusters from later summer through fall. Some are mounded dwarfs that grow 18 to 24 inches tall and wide; others are columnar giants that grow 6 feet tall and half as wide. Especially these larger kinds prove excellent among shrubs or bigger perennials. New England aster (*A. novae-angliae*) grows fast and spreads by shallow rhizomes. It is an excellent fall-flowering alternative to chrysanthemums.

A word about names: Don't confuse these plants with annual asters, which are also called China asters, *Callistephus chinensis*. They bear little resemblance to true asters beyond the shared name. Botanists have recently reassigned most of the native asters to the genus *Symphyotrichum*, a change that most of the horticultural world has so far ignored.

Care: Any garden soil that is relatively moist and well-drained is acceptable, but a rich, amended soil will support superior growth. Pinch new growth in late spring or early summer to force branching that results in more flowers, and then deadhead once many fade to prolong bloom. The tallest kinds need the support of a stake to look their best. Shorter, more compact varieties look neater on their own. Cold-climate gardeners should avoid selecting late-blooming varieties, which might not flower before frost. Wait until spring to clean up plantings so that birds can forage on the seeds. Divide plants every two to three years in spring to control spread and renew plant vigor, discarding the oldest, center section.

Recommended plants and related species: New England aster 'Alma Pötschke' has red-violet blooms on 3- to 4-feet-tall plants. *A. n.* 'Purple Dome' has deep blue flowers on a compact, 1½- to 2-feet-tall plant. New York aster (*A. novi-belgii*) has slightly larger flowers. The hybrid *A.* ×*frikartii* 'Mönch' grows 2½ to 3 feet tall and produces lavender-blue flowers.

New York aster

Astilbe
Astilbe

- **Hardiness Zones: 4–8**
- **Heat Zones: 9–1**
- **Light: Half sun to shade; tolerates sun if soil is constantly moist**
- **Size: 2–4'H×2'W**
- **Features: White, pink, red, or mauve flowers, early to midsummer**

A cluster of several astilbe cultivars

If your garden includes an area of moist soil that is often shaded, and hot summers are not a standard feature, add astilbe to your short list of perennials to plant. There are innumerable varieties that come in many colors, and all are showy, trouble free, and long lived.

Considered individually the flowers are minuscule and barely worth mentioning. But they come by the thousands, on elongated, 6- to 24-inch-tall branched stalks, usually shaped like a compact steeple but sometimes in a loose, drooping plume. Either way they create a considerable show.

Leaves are glossy dark green to nearly bronze and divided into several leaflets, each of which has a toothed edge. The overall effect is of a ferny mound of foliage.

Plant astilbe near ponds, pools, or creeks, or wherever water is implied. Shorter varieties also perform well lining a pathway or in a container.

Astilbe 'Ostrich Plume'

Care: Astilbe grows best in soil that is rich in both nutrients and organic matter. However, moisture is the limiting factor. Astilbe tolerates many soil types and a wide soil pH range. Fertilize generously with compost or manures, and maintain mulch on soil around plants.

Cut plants back in early spring or late fall. They rarely need division, but to obtain more plants, divide in spring or fall. Use a sharp tool to cut the woody crown into sections, each one with several eyes.

Recommended plants and related species: Extensive crossbreeding of astilbe has left most of the original species and relationships useless. So botanists have placed them in groups according to their dominant parentage. 'Bridal Veil' (Arendsii Group) is 2 to 3 feet tall with pinkish white flowers. Early-flowering 'Fanal' (Arendsii Group) grows 2 feet tall and has dark red flowers above bronze leaves. 'Federsee' (Arendsii Group) flowers are carmine on 24-inch-long panicles, and plants are tolerant of dry soil. 'Ostrich Plume' (Thunbergii Group) has pink flowers on 2-feet-tall plants. 'Sprite' star astilbe (Simplicifolia Group) has open plumes of pink and grows up to 12 inches. Chinese astilbe (*A. chinensis*) is a late-summer bloomer; it tolerates drier conditions. *A. c.* 'Pumila' grows 8-plus inches and has mauve-pink blossoms. Flowers of *A. c.* var. *taquetii* reach up to 5 feet tall.

Astilbe chinensis **var. taquetii**

Astrantia major
Great masterwort

- **Hardiness Zones: 4–7**
- **Heat Zones: 8–4**
- **Light: Half to full sun; increase water in full sun**
- **Size: 24–36"H×18"W**
- **Features: White, pink, or rose flowers, late spring to early summer**

Great masterwort 'Alba'

A charming addition to a cottage garden, great masterwort grows 2 to 3 feet tall and produces white, rose, or pink flowers in clusters on top of wiry, branched stems. Like astilbe, plants are hardy and resilient given shade and moisture. But where days are hot and nights warm, plants struggle. Plants form a dense, slowly spreading clump that combines beautifully with pink astilbe, hosta, Siberian iris, or perennial flax.

Care: Plant in rich, well-drained loam that includes plenty of organic matter. Plants do not tolerate drought or hot summer nights. Fertilize generously. Deadhead for prolonged and repeat bloom. Without deadheading, great masterwort may self-sow but not to nuisance levels. Cut back foliage in late fall or early spring. Plants are pest free, but rabbits and groundhogs will occasionally browse them.

Recommended plants and related species: 'Alba' produces white flowers on 2-foot stems. 'Lars' is a vigorous variety with dark red flowers. 'Primadonna' has purple blooms on 30-inch-tall plants.

Athyrium niponicum var. *pictum*
Japanese painted fern

- **Hardiness Zones:** 3–8
- **Heat Zones:** Not determined
- **Light:** Shade
- **Size:** 18"H×15"W
- **Features:** Silvery purple fronds

Japanese painted fern

Japanese painted fern is one of the hardiest and easiest ferns to grow for home gardens. Varieties of ferns with colorful fronds are most popular, and this one is notable for its soft, almost metallic gray color with overtones of red and blue. Combine it with primrose or dwarf Chinese astilbe.
Care: Plant in humus-rich soil, ensure that the soil remains moist, and mulch. The plant thrives in full shade but develops its best color in filtered light. Plant 1 foot apart for colorful ground cover, 2 feet apart for accent.
Recommended plants and related species: A related plant, lady fern (*A. filix-femina*), is larger, reaching 3 feet tall. It is more tolerant of dry soil, but slightly less hardy, to Zone 4. Lady fern is particularly beautiful in spring as its new fronds unfurl.

Aurinia saxatilis
Basket-of-gold

- **Hardiness Zones:** 3–7
- **Heat Zones:** 9–2
- **Light:** Sun or partial shade
- **Size:** 3–15"H×18"W
- **Features:** Brilliant yellow blossoms, spring

In early spring tiny golden flowers completely cover low-growing plants with gray-green foliage. Basket-of-gold struggles in hot, humid areas and is often short-lived. It is useful in front of borders or in rock gardens and is especially attractive spilling over rock walls, raised beds, or containers. The plant pairs particularly well with 'Homestead Purple' verbena.
Care: Plant basket-of-gold in well-drained soil and a sunny location. Set plants about 8 to 12 inches apart. Cut plants back after flowering. Water only during extended periods of drought and hold off on fertilizing. Division in the fall is the easiest method of propagation.
Recommended plants and related species: 'Citrina' is 10 to 15 inches tall with lemon yellow flowers. 'Dudley Nevill' grows to 10 inches tall and has buff-colored flowers; there is also a variegated version called 'Dudley Nevill Variegated'. 'Tom Thumb' is only 3 to 6 inches tall but a vigorous selection.

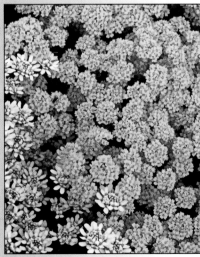

Basket-of-gold

Baptisia australis
Blue false indigo

- **Hardiness Zones:** 4–9
- **Heat Zones:** 9–2
- **Light:** Full to half sun
- **Size:** 3–4'H×4'W
- **Features:** Blue, purple, or white flowers, midspring

Blue false indigo

Count on this easy-to-grow, long-lived North American native to serve as a colorful plant for your garden. A possible anchor plant, blue false indigo is often used toward the back of a border where it will become more robust each year. The tall flower spikes that come in spring will over time multiply in number. After they fade, decorative seedpods remain.
Care: Plant blue false indigo in deep, well-drained soil that is rich in organic matter. Space plants 3½ feet apart in neutral or acid soil of average fertility. Water in dry weather until plants become established. In partial shade, use stakes that the plant can grow through for support. Cut back plants in late fall or early spring.
Recommended plants and related species: 'Purple Smoke' is a hybrid that grows 3 to 4 feet tall. It has charcoal green stems and pale lilac flowers; it is hardy in Zones 3 to 8. White wild indigo, *B. alba*, grows 2 to 3 feet tall and has a 3-foot spread.

Bergenia cordifolia
Heart-leaf bergenia

- **Hardiness Zones: 4–8**
- **Heat Zones: 8–1**
- **Light: Full sun in North, half sun or afternoon shade in South**
- **Size: 1'H×1'W**
- **Features: Unusual foliage adds textural interest**

Heart-leaf bergenia

Heart-leaf bergenia is admired for its bold-texture clumps of cabbagelike leaves and its pink flowers. The 12-inch-long, round to heart-shape leaves have a leathery texture and are evergreen in most climates, semievergreen in the coldest ones. In winter, leaves often take on reddish hues. Irregular flower clusters are held above the leaves on thick stalks. Plants spread slowly by rhizomes.
Care: Plant heart-leaf bergenia in rich, well-drained soil. Plants can survive in dry soil but won't look their best. Space plants 12 to 18 inches apart. Divide them if they become crowded.
Recommended plants and related species: 'Perfect' has round leaves, deep pink flowers on 18-inch stems, and is a zone hardier than the species. 'Evening Glow' has red-purple flowers and maroon leaves in winter. Hybrids include 'Bressingham White' (pink flowers that turn white), and 'Bressingham Ruby' (pink flowers).

Boltonia asteroides
Boltonia

- **Hardiness Zones: 4–9**
- **Heat Zones: 9–2**
- **Light: Full sun to half shade**
- **Size: 5'H×3'W**
- **Features: Profuse white and pink daisylike flowers, fall**

With its frothy stand of yellow-centered, late-season, 1-inch-wide daisies, boltonia could be mistaken for an aster. However, it grows better in hot-summer regions than aster. It's a good partner for other late bloomers, such as Russian sage, hybrid anemone, and ornamental grasses.
Care: Boltonia thrives in any soil but performs best in well-drained soil of average fertility. Space plants 2 to 3 feet apart. Plants seldom need staking despite boltonia's impressive 4- or 5-foot height. In hot regions, plants do better if they are planted in some shade, but staking may then be required. Or cut plants back to 12 inches in late spring, which shortens plants and makes them bushier. Divide plants every three or four years. Boltonia resists mildew.
Recommended plants and related species: 'Pink Beauty' sports lavender-pink blossoms with silver-blue foliage. 'Snowbank' has extra-sturdy stems, snowy white flowers, and blue-green leaves.

Boltonia 'Snowbank'

Brunnera macrophylla
Brunnera

- **Hardiness Zones: 3–7**
- **Heat Zones: 9–3**
- **Light: Shade to dense shade**
- **Size: 18"H×24"W**
- **Features: An airy froth of sky blue flowers, early to midspring**

Brunnera

The joy of brunnera is the springtime cloud of tiny blue flowers that hovers above its heart-shape leaves. The dark green, coarse-texture foliage is a good partner for blue-green plants that are lacy, ferny, and upright, such as fringed bleeding heart, Kamchatka bugbane, astilbe, perennial flax, and jacob's ladder.
Care: Plant in moist, well-drained soil. Brunnera scorches in hot, sunny sites; variegated cultivars are especially prone to this. Plants tolerate full sun only where summers are cool and moisture steady. Cut spent blooms back to the leaves. This prevents self-sowing, which is fine unless you're trying to sustain a cultivar that has variegated leaves. Dig out excess plants and seedlings annually; try to get all their roots. Divide plants as needed every four to five years.
Recommended plants and related species: 'Looking Glass' boasts huge, silver leaves. 'Jack Frost' leaves are silver with darker veins.

Calamagrostis × acutiflora
Feather reed grass

- **Hardiness Zones:** 4–9
- **Heat Zones:** 9–1
- **Light:** Full sun
- **Size:** 3–6'H×2'W
- **Features:** Strong vertical effect, showy foliage, feathery flower stalks

Feather reed grass

Stiffly upright, this cool-season clumping grass changes its look and character through the season. Spring brings a fountain of pale green leaves, which by early summer is topped with tall, feathery, pink flower spikes. These change to light purple in early summer, then ripen into golden wheatlike sheaves by midsummer. The seedheads remain attractive into fall. Feather reed grass is a good companion for black-eyed susan or sedum, for beauty that lasts well into winter.

Care: Best in ordinary well-drained soil. But feather reed grass is also one of the few grasses that will thrive in wet clay soil. Space plants 2 feet apart. Divide crowded clumps in spring after new growth begins. Cut plants back in late winter or spring. Plants tolerate seaside conditions.

Recommended plants and related species: 'Karl Foerster' ('Stricta'), grows 4 to 5 feet tall and blooms in early summer. 'Overdam' (2 to 3 feet tall) and 'Avalanche' (4 feet tall) have white-striped foliage.

Caltha palustris
Marsh marigold

- **Hardiness Zones:** 5–7
- **Heat Zones:** 7–3
- **Light:** Full sun or partial shade
- **Size:** 1'H×1'W
- **Features:** Bright yellow spring blossoms

Marsh marigold is a wetland native that forms attractive, 1-foot-tall clumps of rounded, kidney-shape leaves (which get smaller as they progress up the stem) topped with 1- to 2-inch yellow flowers. Marsh marigold often goes dormant after it blooms. This plant is ideal for low-lying spots where water stands, for the edge of streams, and around water gardens. Combine it with Japanese iris and other perennials that grow in wet soil.

Care: Plant marsh marigold in full sun or partial shade, in wet soil. Or plant underwater so the crown is no more than one inch from the surface. If plants become crowded, divide them during their summer dormancy.

Recommended plants and related species: 'Pleno' (also known as 'Multiplex' or *C. p. flore pleno*) is an outstanding double form with 2-inch-wide yellow flowers. *C. p. alba* has brilliant white single blooms that contrast strikingly with the shiny foliage; however, it is much more difficult to obtain.

Marsh marigold

Campanula
Bellflower

- **Hardiness Zones:** 3–8
- **Heat Zones:** 9–1
- **Light:** Full to half sun
- **Size:** 9–36"H×15"W
- **Features:** Violet, blue-violet, or white bells, late spring to midsummer

Carpathian bellflower with geranium

Bellflowers are among the finest of perennials. They vary from short, diminutive ground-huggers to tall upright plants. All have bell-shape flowers, which may turn up or down.

Care: Plant bellflowers in any soil that is well-drained and moist. They do not tolerate drought, full shade, hot summer nights, or excessively wet soil. Plants may self-sow, and if yours do, named varieties are likely to come true from seed, a garden rarity. Deadhead to prolong bloom and promote repeat bloom. Divide plants in fall or spring every three to five years or when clumps begin to open in the center; they are easy to move. Stake taller varieties. Avoid cutting back in late fall or early spring, unless slugs and snails are a problem. Unfortunately, the plants attract rabbits and woodchucks.

Recommended plants and related species: Carpathian bellflower (*C. carpatica*) is a 9- to 12-inch-tall mound that serves well toward the front of borders or as an edging; it blooms in late spring to early summer. Cultivars include: 'Bressingham White' and 'White Clips' with white flowers, and 'Blue Moonlight' and 'Blue Clips' with blue flowers.

Clustered bellflower

Clustered bellflower (*C. glomerata*) has white or violet flowers in early summer; it is 12 to 36 inches tall. Cut it back hard after bloom. The cultivar 'Superba' is notably heat tolerant.

Milky bellflower (*C. lactiflora*) has violet, pink, or white blooms on 3-foot-tall stems in midsummer. Most varieties will fall over without support, so place stakes early in the season. The dwarf cultivar 'Pouffe' grows to only 18 inches, so it doesn't need support.

Peach-leaf bellflower (*C. persicifolia*) has white, pink, or violet out-turned bells on wiry stems above attractive foliage. Cut stems are excellent in arrangements. Plants spread vigorously but are less heat tolerant than others. 'Telham Beauty' has 3-inch-wide blue flowers on slender stalks.

Carex
Sedge

- **Hardiness Zones: 5–9**
- **Heat Zones: 12–1**
- **Light: Shade in hot areas; sun in areas with cool summers**
- **Size: 1–2'H×1–2'W**
- **Features: Handsome foliage**

Sedge's colorful foliage is evergreen in hot regions, semievergreen in colder ones. It grows in clumps and has a low, arching form. This compact grass look-alike is an excellent choice for shady borders, and in Southern gardens will supply year-round beauty and interest. It is pretty as an accent, in masses, or as an edging. Growth becomes denser with time.

Care: Plant in moist, well-drained soil and in full or partial shade in hot areas, sun in cold areas. Space 18 inches apart. Avoid overwatering, and let plants die to the ground in fall. Cut back the previous year's foliage in spring.

Recommended plants and related species: Variegated Japanese sedge (*Carex morrowii* 'Variegata') has silvery variegated foliage. Handsome 'Bowles Golden' tufted sedge (*C. elata*) is 24 inches tall with bright golden yellow leaves that have thin green margins. 'Aurea' has green leaves with a yellow margin. The yellow color of leaf blades fades as summer temperatures rise.

Tufted sedge 'Bowles Golden'

Catananche caerulea
Cupid's dart

- **Hardiness Zones: 4–7**
- **Heat Zones: 9–1**
- **Light: Full sun**
- **Size: 2'H×1'W**
- **Features: Light blue flowers, summer to early fall**

Cupid's dart

Cupid's dart has papery blue flowers with a dark eye on wiry stems. Leaves form a rosette of narrow gray-green foliage that hugs the ground; in bloom, the flower stems rise to 24 inches. Plants grow quickly in clumps.

Care: Plant in well-drained, sandy soil. Heat-, drought-, and wind-tolerant, cupid's dart does not grow well in high heat combined with high humidity. Plants are short-lived, though usually pest free. Deadhead to prolong bloom. No need to cut down cupid's dart in late fall or early spring, because stems and foliage decompose rapidly over winter. Divide plants every two to three years to promote new growth.

Recommended plants and related species: For white flowers, grow the cultivar 'Alba'. Be careful with cupid's dart: it has figured prominently in love potions for generations. The genus name stems from a Greek word that translates as "powerful incentive."

Centaurea montana
Mountain bluet

- **Hardiness Zones: 3–8**
- **Heat Zones: 9–1**
- **Light: Full to half sun**
- **Size: 15–24"H×24"W**
- **Features: Blue-violet blooms with reddish center**

Mountain bluet

The mounded, gray-green plants grow to about 15 inches tall and are topped by lacy flowers on leafy 24-inch stems. Plants spread by both seeds and stolons, aggressively in cool northern regions where the species is best adapted. Blooms are 2 inches or more across with wisps radiating from a darker center. Downy foliage fills in around the tall, narrow plants.
Care: Once established in well-drained soil, plants take wind, heat, drought, and high pH in stride. Cut them back hard after spring bloom to promote lush new foliage and to prevent self-sowing. Cut-back plants may bloom a second time in summer. Divide as necessary, every three years or so. If plants are grown in shade, flower stems will stretch and flop over unless staked.
Recommended plants and related species: 'Alba' has white flowers; those of 'Grandiflora' are blue but larger. Persian cornflower *(C. dealbata)* is a 24- to 36-inch-tall pink-flowering relative that blooms several weeks later.

Centranthus ruber
Centranthus

- **Hardiness Zones: 5–9**
- **Heat Zones: 9–2**
- **Light: Full sun**
- **Size: 2–3'H×2'W**
- **Features: Iridescent reddish pink blooms, summer**

This old-fashioned, bushy plant is indestructible where it's neither too cold nor too humid. Many of California's back roads, where it lives on only what nature provides, are bordered by it. On the other hand, too much chill, too much summer humidity, or soil that is too acidic spell its doom. Each flower is only about ¼ inch long, but there are hundreds in each spike, making the overall impact quite significant. Cut flower spikes look good enough for indoor display.
Care: Plant centranthus in any well-drained, alkaline soil. Set plants 18 to 24 inches apart, and deadhead to promote repeat blooming. Pests are never a problem. Plants are typically short-lived, but they self-sow sparingly, making established plantings long lasting. Divide plants in spring or fall.
Recommended plants and related species: 'Albus' produces ivory-white flowers and 'Coccineus' has deep rose-red blossoms.

Centranthus

Cerastium tomentosum
Snow-in-summer

- **Hardiness Zones: 3–7**
- **Heat Zones: 9–1**
- **Light: Full sun to partial shade**
- **Size: 6–8"H×12"W**
- **Features: Year-round silvery leaves and white flowers in late spring**

Snow-in-summer with New Zealand flax

This plant's common name aptly describes the impression it creates, especially during its late-spring bloom. Squint and you can convince yourself you're seeing snow. And given the silvery, ½-inch-long leaves, the effect doesn't wane completely with the flowers. As a native to the mountains of southern Italy and Sicily, snow-in-summer grows best in mild but cool regions. In the Pacific Northwest, for instance, it's so prolific it's nearly a weed. It has naturalized throughout most of Europe, survives the coldest North American winters, and has the potential to become a weed. Combine it with conifers, or use as an edging or bulb cover.
Care: Plant in any well-drained soil. Heat, humidity, and poor drainage are the plant's limiting factors. Shear off flowers after they fade, to maintain plant vigor. If your situation allows it, set your lawn mower on high and mow it. When bare sections appear, replant divisions taken from a healthy section of the plant.

Ceratostigma plumbaginoides
Leadwort

- Hardiness Zones: 5–9
- Heat Zones: 9–4
- Light: Full sun to partial shade
- Size: 8"H×15"W
- Features: Intense blue flowers, late summer to fall

Leadwort

This low-slung, modestly spreading perennial is perfect for rocky areas. It has masses of gentian blue flowers from summer to late fall, plus red-tinged leaves that turn bronze in autumn for long-lasting seasonal color. Use leadwort to underplant spring-blooming bulbs, to serve as a groundcover in sunny spots, or to ramble over rocks.

Care: Leadwort thrives and spreads rapidly in well-drained, good-quality soil, and will tolerate a wide range of soil types, from clay to sand. In soils that are wet or waterlogged, it does poorly. Space plants 12 inches apart. In areas where plant tops aren't killed by cold, cut them back hard in early spring. Divide in early spring if clumps die out in center. Plants are late to emerge in spring.

Recommended plants and related species: Griffith's leadwort (*C. griffithii*) is similarly handsome, with deep blue flowers and red-margined evergreen foliage. In fall the leaves take on red and yellow hues. Hardy in Zones 6 to 8.

Chasmanthium latifolium
Northern sea oats

- Hardiness Zones: 3–8
- Heat Zones: 12–1
- Light: Full sun or partial shade
- Size: 30–48"H×18"W
- Features: Ornamental grass grown for clusters of seeds

A native of North American woodlands, northern sea oats grows in bamboolike clumps about 18 inches wide and, when in flower, 4 feet tall. Tiny silvery flowers that appear in spring mature into flattened clusters that are green at first but later an attractive bronze. These flowering stems are the plant's most ornamental feature and alone are reason enough to add northern sea oats to your garden. The flower stems are also terrific additions to indoor arrangements. Northern sea oats has the potential to spread, by both seed and runners, especially where the growing season is long and rainy.

Care: Plant in sun or partial shade in rich, well-drained soil. Space 24 inches apart. Divide clumps in order to have more plants or to reinvigorate flowers.

Northern sea oats

Chelone obliqua
Rose turtlehead

- Hardiness Zones: 3–8
- Heat Zones: 9–3
- Light: Dense shade to full sun
- Size: 2–3'H×1'W
- Features: Deep rose-purple flowers, late summer to fall

Rose turtlehead

Rose turtlehead gets its name from its flowers, which resemble the heads of snapping turtles. It is a sturdy, vertical or columnar plant with medium-texture, deep green foliage. It spreads by shallow rhizomes at a moderate rate, forming wide, dense colonies.

Care: Plants prefer a soil that is moist and that has a neutral or slightly acid pH. Where summers are very hot or in full sun, constant moisture is essential. Fertilize generously. To keep turtlehead in check near less aggressive plants, reduce the colony in spring each year. Pinch plants several times between midspring and midsummer to reduce height at flowering; deadheading is not needed. Cut plants back in late fall or early spring, and divide them every four to five years.

Recommended plants and related species: 'Bethelii' produces more flowers that are more deeply rose colored. White-flowered 'Alba' is slower growing.

Chrysanthemum
Chrysanthemum

- **Hardiness Zones: varies by species**
- **Heat Zones: varies by species**
- **Light: Full to half sun**
- **Size: 1–4'H×1–4'W**
- **Features: All colors except blue, late summer and fall**

Florist's chrysanthemum

These are ancient garden plants that have been intensively cultivated in Asia for at least 2,500 years. In part as a consequence of their antiquity, there are numerous hybrids of unknown or mixed up parentage. So their names, which are supposed to bear some relation to their botany, are similarly mixed up, especially in recent years. This is sorted out briefly below.

All chrysanthemums are daisies, and most bloom in mid- to late summer and fall, depending on the variety and your region.

Care: Plant chrysanthemums in moist, rich, and well-drained soil, and fertilize generously. They do not tolerate wet soil but will grow well in windy locations if they have plenty of moisture. Pinch several times between midspring and midsummer for short, bushy, later-blooming plants. Northern gardeners should stop pinching by mid-July; Southern gardeners, by early August. Unpinched plants may need staking. In Zones 5 to 6

wait until early spring to cut back plants. Or cut them down in fall and cover roots with mulch over winter. Poor drainage affects hardiness. Divide plants every two years in spring to keep clumps vigorous. Replant divisions in a different location to prevent pest buildup. Aphids, Japanese beetles, mites, slugs, snails, and nematodes can be problems. Leaf spot, mildew, and rust infect older, crowded clumps. Rabbits, deer, and groundhogs graze on plants.

Recommended plants and related species: Most hybrid chrysanthemums are now placed in one of three groups—the Indicum, Koreanum, or Rubellum —to broadly indicate the variety's heritage.

Some related species have been moved to other genera. For example, shasta daisy was *Chrysanthemum ×superbum,* but is now *Leucanthemum.* You can read about it on page 95.

Fall or florist's chrysanthemums belong to the Indicum Group. You can plant them in the garden, but they may not flower in northern regions because they've been bred to flower only after a very specific sequence of hours of darkness. There is an abundance of cultivars in this group.

'Clara Curtis', Rubellum Group, (formerly *C. ×rubellum)* grows about 3 feet high and wide. Pink to red flowers are about 2 inches

Painted daisy

across and produced in profusion in autumn.

Reclassified chrysanthemums: White marguerite daisy *(Argyranthemum frutescens,* formerly *C. frutescens)* has fine-texture, light green leaves. It grows in Zones 9 to 11 and is particularly favored as a plant for containers.

Marguerite daisy

Silver and gold *(Ajania pacifica,* formerly *C. pacificum* and *Dendranthema pacifica)* is grown for its light green leaves that are outlined in silver. At about 2 feet tall and wide it serves well in perennial borders. It's hardy in Zones 6 to 9.

Montauk daisy *(Nipponanthemum nipponicum,* formerly *C. nipponicum)* is a semievergreen woody perennial that grows 2 to 3 feet tall and produces clouds of white daisies in fall. It tolerates wind and salt in Zones 5 to 9. Avoid pinching in Zones 5 to 6.

Painted daisy *(Tanacetum coccineum,* formerly *C. coccineum)* grows about 2 feet tall, half as wide, and has 2- to 3-inch-diameter red or white flowers with yellow centers. It's hardy in Zones 3 to 7, and heat Zones 12 to 1.

Feverfew *(Tanacetum parthenium,* formerly *C. parthenium)* grows 3 feet high and 2 feet wide and produces white and yellow flowers in late summer. Plants are hardy in Zones 5 to 7, and in Heat Zones 12 to 1.

Chrysogonum virginianum
Goldenstar

- **Hardiness Zones:** 5–8
- **Heat Zones:** 9–2
- **Light:** Full sun or partial shade
- **Size:** 6–8"H×12"W
- **Features:** Bright yellow daisy flowers in early spring

Goldenstar

Goldenstar is a modest plant but one that has great charm. Its 1-inch-diameter bright yellow flowers cover the mat of dark green leaves in May, then retreat into sporadic bloom for the remainder of the season. Flowering is more consistent in cool weather, and summer heat spells stop flowers altogether. Leaves are 1 to 2 inches long and have a delicately toothed or scalloped edge.
Care: Plant in moist, well-drained soil in a place that receives afternoon shade. If your climate has cool summers, full sun is OK. Space plants about 12 inches apart. Propagate by division or seed.
Recommended plants and related species: 'Alan Bush' is somewhat more robust and flowerful than the species. 'Eco Lacquered Spider' has grayish leaves and the capacity to spread very fast.

Convallaria majalis
Lily-of-the-valley

- **Hardiness Zones:** 3–8
- **Heat Zones:** 9–1
- **Light:** Shade to dense shade
- **Size:** 6"H×6"W
- **Features:** Fragrant, bell-shaped white or pink flowers, spring

In spring, this dense, fragrant perennial has stalks of sweet-scented bell-shape flowers with scalloped edges. Most lilies-of-the-valley have single snow-white flowers, but there are some cultivars with double flowers and some with pink blooms. Some varieties have variegated leaves. Use lily-of-the-valley in shady areas under trees and shrubs, but be wary of its capacity to spread.
Care: Lily-of-the-valley thrives and spreads rapidly in moist soil. In dry soil, it survives well but does not spread. Heat also slows the spread of the plants. Space plants 6 to 12 inches apart. Water them well throughout the year. Fertilize in fall after the first frost. In colder regions, protect plants from severe winter weather by covering beds with mulch in fall. Propagate lily-of-the-valley by division. Fruits are poisonous.

Lily-of-the-valley

Coreopsis
Coreopsis

- **Hardiness Zones:** 4–9
- **Heat Zones:** 9–1
- **Light:** Full sun to partial shade
- **Size:** 1–3'H×1–2'W
- **Features:** Daisylike flowers, early to midsummer

Threadleaf coreopsis 'Moonbeam'

The creamy golden yellow daisies of coreopsis light up perennial gardens. Some cultivars are short and mounded; others are loosely columnar. Plants grow quickly.
Care: Coreopsis tolerates drought and alkaline soil but not wet soil. Cut back hard after the first flowering to stimulate further bloom. In late fall or early spring, cut plants back to the ground. Divide plants every two to three years to maintain vigor. Coreopsis spread by offsets and plants are easy to move. This plant is basically pest free.
Recommended plants and related species: 'Moonbeam' threadleaf coreopsis (C. verticillata) is a standout. Its dainty pale yellow flowers appear from summer to frost on 10- to 12-inch-tall mounds of fine-textured leaves. New cultivars of pink coreopsis (C. rosea) are 'Sweet Dreams' (pink with a dark center), and 'Crème Brûleé' (flowers that rise above leaves). Lanceleaf coreopsis (C. lanceolata) grows 2 feet tall and has 2½ inch-diameter daisies on long, slender stalks.

Corydalis lutea
Yellow corydalis

- **Hardiness Zones: 5–7**
- **Heat Zones: 8–3**
- **Light: Half sun to dense shade**
- **Size: 15"H×18"W**
- **Features: Butter yellow flowers, spring to summer**

Yellow corydalis

In the regions where it is hardy, and in the right, moist, woodlandlike situation, yellow corydalis is the perfect perennial. Blue-green, 1- to 4-inch-long divided leaves have a delicate ferny look that is reminiscent of bleeding heart, to which the plant is related. Golden yellow flowers are small, about ¾ inches long, and bloom on wiry stems in clusters, straight through summer. The overall effect is totally charming. In the Pacific Northwest, perfect conditions for yellow corydalis prevail, and the plant is nearly a weed. Plants grow quickly and spread by reseeding.
Care: Ideal soil for yellow corydalis is moist, well-drained, and slightly alkaline. Full sun is OK if the soil is cool and constantly moist. But even so, foliage and flower colors will bleach out somewhat. There is no need to deadhead yellow corydalis; it would be quite a chore, since the plants bear many flowers freely over a long period. Plants self-sow, but the seedlings are easily weeded out if you desire. If you buy plants, be careful of their delicate stems that are easily broken. Propagate by dividing clumps or sowing seed in spring or fall. Packaged seed is difficult to germinate. It is better to find an existing planting and collect seed from it. Fresh seed germinates readily the following spring if sown immediately after collection. Or get seedlings from gardening friends. Plants are pest free.
Recommended plants and related species: Blue corydalis (*C. flexuosa*) is about the same size as yellow corydalis, but is slightly more heat tolerant (to Zone 8) and has smoky blue flowers. It is striking in cool, fertile, shaded areas. Unlike yellow corydalis, it goes dormant in summer. 'Blue Panda' has sky blue flowers.

Blue corydalis

Crocosmia × crocosmiiflora
Crocosmia

- **Hardiness Zones: 5–9**
- **Heat Zones: 9–6**
- **Light: Full to half sun**
- **Size: 2–3'H×1'W**
- **Features: Red-orange or yellow flowers, midsummer**

Crocosmia

Crocosmia lights up a midsummer border with glowing flowers that line the arching tip of each stem. Its swordlike foliage grows in a vase-shape clump. Plants spread at a moderate pace by short rhizomes from gladioluslike corms.
Care: Crocosmia does not tolerate wet soil or drought. Clip off the entire flowering stem after the last bud opens and fades. Divide plants in spring every three years. Plants may require staking if growing in part shade. Crocosmia is sometimes listed as hardy to Zone 6, but winter losses in Zone 5 likely result from poor drainage. Older plants with larger roots are hardier. Cover new plants with a thick mulch for the first few winters until the plants are full size.
Recommended plants and related species: Several hybrids are available. Some of the best are: 'Emily McKenzie' (dark orange); 'Jenny Bloom' (yellow); 'Venus' (yellow pink, compact); 'Vulcan' (deep red-orange, hardy); and 'Lucifer' (bright red).

Delosperma
Ice plant

- **Hardiness Zones: 5–10**
- **Heat Zones: 10–7**
- **Light: Sun to half shade**
- **Size: 3–4"H×24"W**
- **Features: Yellow to deep purple blooms, winter and summer**

Hardy ice plant

Ice plant grows close to the ground and provides a quick, thick cover. Its succulent green leaves appear different depending on the species or variety and whether or not it's grown in shade or sun. Plants have daisylike flowers in colors ranging from yellow to deep purple to red. Plants may bloom in winter and again in summer, often producing flowers sporadically.

Care: Plant in a sunny area and well-drained soil. Propagate plants from cuttings or division. Space them 4 to 6 inches apart.

Recommended plants and related species: Purple ice plant (*D. cooperi*) has 2-inch purple blooms on 6-inch-tall plants. Hardy ice plant (*D. nubigenum*) has 1-inch-diameter yellow flowers and emerald green foliage that turns red in fall. It grows to 2 to 3 inches tall and 3 feet wide. All are hardy to Zone 5.

Delphinium elatum
Hybrid bee delphinium

- **Hardiness Zones: 3–7**
- **Heat Zones: 6–1**
- **Light: Full to half sun**
- **Size: 3–6'H (in bloom)×2–3'W**
- **Features: Blue, violet, pink, white, or two-toned flowers, early to midsummer**

Tall, flowering wands top the 18-inch mound of delphinium foliage in spring and early summer. Plants develop a 3- to 6-feet-tall spike of flowers that is a perennial garden showstopper. Combine delphinium with later-blooming tall plants: joe-pye weed, anise hyssop, ornamental grasses, New York ironweed, or culver's root. In bloom, hybrid bee delphinium complements queen-of-the-prairie and meadow rue.

Care: Plant these delphiniums in moist, rich, and well-drained soil. They do not tolerate wind, heat, drought, or poorly drained soil. Afternoon shade is usually preferred. Fertilize generously. Deadhead plants to prolong flowering. Remove the entire flowering stalk, cutting it just above a large leaf low on that stem. New flowering shoots will develop from the stem. After the second bloom, cut the flower

Hybrid bee delphinium, Pacific Giant Group

stems back to the basal leaves. Water and fertilize, then wait for new basal shoots to emerge and old foliage to wither. Then remove the old stalks. Thin the shoots on established plants in early spring; allow just five to seven shoots per clump. Stake stems individually, tying them at 12-inch intervals.

Hybrid bee delphinium, Belladonna Group

Divide delphiniums every three years in early fall; they have offsets. Grow the new plants in beds that have not held delphiniums for several years. This delphinium grows from seed or stem cuttings taken in spring and rooted in water. Cut plants down in late fall and remove all the foliage to reduce pest problems. Leaf spot, powdery mildew, and stem and crown rot can pose problems, as can slugs, snails, and stalk borer. Remove and destroy all discolored foliage and flowers. Avoid crowding plants.

Recommended plants and related species: Given the many recent years of intensive delphinium hybridization that have occurred, there are numerous cultivars, series, and groups. The Pacific Giant Group, which boasts showy spikes of clear, brightly colored double flowers, is among the tallest. Clear white 'Galahad' is an example. Plants in the Magic Fountain strain are similar, but half the height. The Belladonna Group has loose, multiple flower stalks and is more heat-tolerant.

Dennstaedtia punctilobata
Hay-scented fern

- **Hardiness Zones: 2–8**
- **Heat Zones: 8–1**
- **Light: Shade to dense shade**
- **Size: 2–3'H×2'W**
- **Features: Grown for yellow-green fronds**

Hay-scented fern

The dried or crushed yellow-green fronds of this North American native fern smell like crushed hay, which is the source of the name. The beautiful hairy, arching fronds have a lacy texture and grow 2 to 3 feet tall. This easy-to-grow fern tolerates a wide range of conditions. Use it to provide groundcover in a shady border. In autumn the fronds turn a soft shade of yellow.

Care: Hay-scented fern grows best in partial to deep shade in rich, moist, well-drained acid soil, but will tolerate open sun and a wide range of soil conditions. Once established, plants can survive in fairly dry soil. Plant them 3 feet apart. Hay-scented fern may become too invasive for the small garden, but it is attractive and care-free in large gardens where it has room to roam. It spreads by rhizomes. Slugs and snails may be a problem.

Deschampsia caespitosa
Tufted hair grass

- **Hardiness Zones: 4–8**
- **Heat Zones: 9–1**
- **Light: Sun to half sun**
- **Size: 2'H×3'W**
- **Features: An ornamental grass with fine, thin blades and creamy plumes in late summer**

This graceful grass of glistening, silver-tinged purple spikelets sprouts long-lasting frothy flowers in late summer. It is an excellent choice for the woodland garden. This fine-texture grass provides year-round interest and is especially attractive with hostas or ferns. In mild-winter areas, flower stems turn bronzy yellow and foliage stays evergreen.

Care: Space plants 18 inches apart. They grow best in partial shade and damp soil but adjust to varied situations. However, tufted hair grass does not perform well in hot, humid conditions. Where soil is dry, work in organic matter before planting. Comb or rake out the previous year's leaves before new growth begins in spring.

Recommended plants and related species: 'Bronze Veil' grows 2 to 3 feet tall with bronze-yellow tinted flowers and a high heat tolerance. 'Golden Pendant' has dark green leaves and spikelets that age to a rich golden yellow.

Tufted hair grass

Diascia hybrid
Twinspur

- **Hardiness Zones: 8–9**
- **Heat Zones: 4–1**
- **Light: Sun or shade**
- **Size: 1'H×1'W**
- **Features: Pink blooms, spring, early summer, and fall**

Twinspur 'Wink Lavender Pink'

The diminutive (1 inch or less) flowers of twinspur bloom in showy clusters on low clumps. In mild and cool climates, twinspur puts on a show in early summer and fall. It makes a good container plant in cold climates.

Care: Grow twinspur in sun or partial shade in rich, moist, well-drained soil, 15 inches apart. Water to keep moist, but take care not to overwater. Twinspur does not do well in either heat or humidity. Take cuttings to ensure survival. In the South, plant in the fall and enjoy the flowers in the spring.

Recommended plants and related species: 'Ruby Field' barber's twinspur *(D. barberae)* is the most popular hybrid. It grows 10 to 12 inches tall with rose-color flowers. Among hybrid cultivars 'Wink Lavender Pink' has lilac-color flowers, and 'Blackthorn Apricot' has apricot-color flowers; both cultivars reach 12 inches high. Rigid twinspur *(D. rigescens)* grows 1 to 2 feet tall, with 6- to 8-inch-long trusses of spurred, rosy pink flowers.

Dianthus
Pinks

- **Hardiness Zones: 4–8**
- **Heat Zones: 9–1**
- **Light: Half to full sun**
- **Size: 2–30"H×2–15"W, depending on species**
- **Features: Colorful flowers in late spring to early summer**

Dianthus 'Firewitch'

Pinks are an old-fashioned favorite, ideal for the cottage garden, the rock garden, or border front. This group includes plants from tiny creepers to 30-inch-tall cut flowers. Taller varieties are superb for cutting. Pinks have small, frilly, fragrant blossoms in all colors and combinations except blue. Flowers may be single, semidouble, or double. The plant forms a mound of grassy foliage. Combine pinks' grassy, silvery, blue-green foliage with coarser front-of-the-border plants, such as geranium, white sage, coral bells, dwarf bearded iris, and meadow sage. Pinks bloom at the same time as perennial bachelor's button, 'May Queen' ox-eye daisy, and gas plant.

Care: Pinks do not tolerate wet soil or pH below 6. They take heat and drought, but not heat and high humidity. Fertilize and water plants well throughout the growing season for repeat bloom in late summer or fall where nights are cool. Deadhead to prolong bloom; flowers are on branched stems. Divide plants every two to three years; they have offsets. Pinks attract rabbits. Leaf spot can be a problem where soil is moist, humidity high, and air circulation poor. To propagate, pull off stem sections, leaving a bit of woody basal tissue intact (stem cuttings with a "heel"), and root these in early fall. Cut back foliage in early spring, leaving intact the leafy base of woody stems.

Recommended plants and related species: Allwood pinks *(Dianthus ×allwoodii)* are 1- to 1½-foot-tall plants with gray-green foliage. Notable cultivars include 'Aqua', which grows to 12 inches tall and has fragrant white flowers that are doubled. 'Ian' is rich red with a black-red petal edge; it may be hardy only to Zone 5.

Sweet william *(D. barbatus)* is a biennial or short-lived perennial with flat-top flower clusters on 12- to 24-inch stems. It forms loose mats of deep green foliage. Colors range from white to pink to dark red; some are bicolor. 'Blood Red' grows to 15 inches and has the darkest red flower. Encourage self seeding by deadheading when seed pods open, scattering the seeds as you remove the pods.

Cheddar pink

D. caryophyllus is the carnation that florists grow in greenhouses. Available colors include white, pink, red, purple, yellow, and apricot on erect 18- to 30-inch stems in Zones 8 to 10.

Maiden pink *(D. deltoides)* and cheddar pink *(D. gratianopolitanus)* are also more tolerant of summer

Dianthus 'Tiny Rubies'

heat and humidity. They are shorter, mat-forming plants. Cheddar pink cultivars: 'Bath's Pink' is pale pink. 'Firewitch' grows 3 to 4 inches high and flowers to 8 inches. 'Tiny Rubies' has double, deep pink blooms. Both are hardy to Zone 3.

Cultivars of indeterminent parentage include: 'Doris' has a salmon-pink flower with a darker pink center and excellent fragrance. 'Mountain Mist' is rose pink, mat-forming, and more tolerant of heat and humidity than many others. It grows 10 inches tall. 'Mrs Sinkins' was hybridized shortly after the Civil War, and the fact it's still around is testament to its virtues, mainly the double white fragrant flowers on 15-inch-tall plants.

Dicentra spectabilis
Old-fashioned bleeding heart

- **Hardiness Zones:** 3–8
- **Heat Zones:** 7–1
- **Light:** Sun to shade
- **Size:** 18–30"H×36"W
- **Features:** Large pink or white hearts, mid- to late spring

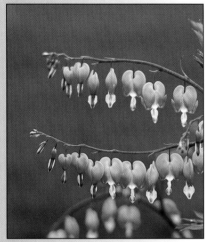

Old-fashioned bleeding heart

Old-fashioned bleeding heart is a clump-forming, slow-growing perennial with deep roots. Outstanding for shade gardens, it has large pink or white flowers that dangle from arching stems.
Care: This plant does not tolerate wet soil. If grown in full sun, dry soil, or high heat, plants go dormant, leaving a large gap in the border. Fertilize generously. There's no need to cut plants back in fall or early spring. Old-fashioned bleeding heart will not flower again without winter cold. Plants rarely need division. Moving them may break brittle roots; plants reestablish slowly. Plants are pest free, and even rabbits, woodchucks, and deer do not browse them.
Recommended plants and related species: 'Pantaloons' is a white cultivar that is notably vigorous. Fringed bleeding heart *(D. eximia)* is an 18-inch-tall relative with finely divided gray-green leaves. The hybrid 'King of Hearts' (dark pink to cherry red flowers) is the longest-blooming cultivar.

Dictamnus albus
Gas plant

- **Hardiness Zones:** 3–9
- **Heat Zones:** 8–1
- **Light:** Full sun to shade
- **Size:** 2–4'H×2–4'W
- **Features:** Starry white or pale rose flowers on tall spikes, midspring

Gas plant is an impressive sight in bloom or later, when its ripe brown seedpods open to form a wand of nut-brown stars. Its starry white or pale rose flowers open on tall spikes over shiny, dark foliage. Flowers and foliage have a sharp lemon fragrance, which is pleasant to some but not others. Plants are clump-forming and slow to expand.
Care: Gas plant does not tolerate poor drainage or hot nights (above 80°F). Either deadhead or leave flower stalks in place for winter interest. The plants rarely need division. Move or divide them in spring or early fall as necessary, or leave in place. Gas plant is pest free though is sometimes a host to black swallowtail and giant swallowtail butterfly larvae. Use care in working around the plant; oil from leaves can cause a burnlike rash.
Recommended plants and related species: The enchanting flowers of purple gas plant *(D. albus* 'Purpureus') are mauve-purple with darker veins.

Purple gas plant

Digitalis purpurea
Common foxglove

- **Hardiness Zones:** 4–9
- **Heat Zones:** 8–3
- **Light:** Shade
- **Size:** 4'H×3'W
- **Features:** Pink, purple, red, white, and yellow flowers, late spring to early summer

Common foxglove

This is a statuesque plant with colorful, bell-shaped flowers for woodland gardens. It is perfect for informal gardens, where foxglove can self-sow with abandon. Actually a biennial, this species self-sows so well you can count on its perennial presence. Leaves of all foxgloves are toxic if ingested.
Care: Plant in partial to deep shade in moist, rich, acid, well-drained soil. Sow seeds outdoors without covering them in late spring or early summer for blooms the following year, or set out plants 18 inches apart in the fall.
Recommended plants and related species: Plants in the Excelsior Group are 5 feet tall; flowers are pink, rose, white, and yellow. 'Foxy' blooms the first year from seed. Treat it as an annual. 'Alba' *(D. purpurea albiflora)* has white blooms. Yellow foxglove *(D. grandiflora)* is perennial, 2 to 3 feet tall with creamy yellow flowers. Perennial strawberry foxglove *(D. ×mertonensis)*, has 2- to 3-foot-tall coppery rose spires. It's hardy in Zone 5 to 9.

Doronicum orientale
Caucasian leopard's bane

- **Hardiness Zones: 4–7**
- **Heat Zones: 12–5**
- **Light: Half sun to shade**
- **Size: 15–24"H×12"W**
- **Features: Cheerful yellow flowers, late spring**

Caucasian leopard's bane

A rare daisy for shade, caucasian leopard's bane has clusters of yellow flowers covering its mound of heart-shape, dark-green leaves. Interplant it with ferns, which will cover up bare spots when the plant goes dormant in summer.
Care: Plant in moist soil that is rich in organic matter. Although caucasian leopard's bane doesn't tolerate heat and goes dormant in summer after it blooms, plants are easy to grow. Space plants 12 to 15 inches apart. Mulch to conserve soil moisture; water during dry weather.
Recommended plants and related species: 'Finesse' has semidouble, yellow-orange flowers on 15-inch stems. 'Magnificum' forms neat, 15-inch-tall mounds with bright yellow flowers on 2½-foot-tall stems. A hybrid cultivar, 'Miss Mason', is 1 to 2 feet tall with canary yellow daisy flowers and more persistent foliage than the species.

Dryopteris filix-mas
Male wood fern

- **Hardiness Zones: 4–8**
- **Heat Zones: Not rated**
- **Light: Shade or half sun**
- **Size: 3–4'H×3'W**
- **Features: Tall, erect fronds with deeply divided leaflets**

Sturdy and robust, this fern grows 4 feet tall. It is a favorite for the shady woodland setting, assuming it has the room to show off. Plants form substantial clumps. They are attractive in the garden combined with Japanese toad lily or bleeding heart.
Care: Plant male wood fern in shade or filtered sun in neutral to acid, fertile soil, spacing plants 2 feet apart. Replenish organic matter. Divide larger clumps regularly. If new plants are not divided, the symmetry of the fern may be lost, and it will become a large clump, which many consider attractive. Fronds are long lasting, and persist well into winter.
Recommended plants and related species: 'Crispa' is a dwarf form with crested fronds. 'Cristata' has divided and crested frond tips. 'Linearis' bears fronds with slender, linear divisions. Autumn fern *(D. erythrosora)* is a colorful evergreen with coppery red new growth that holds its color until fully mature but then changes to a deep glossy green. It's hardy in Zones 5 to 9.

Male wood fern

Echinacea purpurea
Purple coneflower

- **Hardiness Zones: 3–8**
- **Heat Zones: 12–1**
- **Light: Full to half sun**
- **Size: 2–4'H×2'W**
- **Features: Purple or white flowers, early to midsummer**

Purple coneflower

Purple coneflower has daisylike petals that circle a rust-colored central cone. The petals flare back from the cone as the flowers age. These are columnar, coarse-textured, clump-forming, and fast-growing plants.
Care: Plants tolerate heat, wind, humidity, drought, clay soil, and shade. Coneflower self-sows; seedlings vary in height, color, and flower size. Cut back plants in late fall or early spring. Deadhead to prolong bloom into fall. Divide plants every four to five years in fall or spring to maintain vigor. They have offsets and are easy to move. Staking is unnecessary.
Recommended plants and related species: 'Magnus' has larger, darker pink flowers with a less pronounced central cone. Its petals do not droop with maturity. 'Kim's Mophead' and 'Little Giant' are dwarf, 2- to 3-feet-tall cultivars. Intergeneric hybrid Big Sky cultivars, such as 'Big Sky Sunset', have yellows and golds in the flowers. 'Fragrant Angel' is the best white-flower form. They are half the height of the species and slow growing.

Echinops ritro
Globe thistle

- Hardiness Zones: 3–8
- Heat Zones: 12–1
- Light: Full to half sun
- Size: 2–4'H×2'W
- Features: Pale blue flowers, midsummer

Globe thistle

Spheres of steely blue buds in early summer open to pale blue flowers in midsummer. Plants form a strong, coarse column. They are fast growing and clump forming. The coarse gray-green foliage and spherical flowers are a unique addition to gardens.
Care: Plants take drought, heat, and shade. Deadhead to prolong bloom. Cut plants back by one-third to one-half to lateral flower buds. When new basal leaves start to develop and all flowering is finished, remove the spent flowering stems (or leave some for birds). Plants will rebloom in fall in cool, moist seasons. Plants readily self-sow. Globe thistle is basically pest-free. Painted lady caterpillars occasionally knit shoot tips together but cause no real damage. Flowers fade to pale blue in hot weather.
Recommended plants and related species: 'Taplow Blue' has steel blue flowers; 'Veitch's Blue' is darker blue. Russian globe thistle *(E. exaltatus)* is taller, to 8 feet, with silvery white flowers. It attracts birds and butterfly larvae.

Epimedium
Barrenwort

- Hardiness Zones: 4–9
- Heat Zones: 8–5
- Light: Shade to dense shade
- Size: 6–15"H×12"W
- Features: Dainty flowers in early spring; evergreen foliage

The flowers of barrenwort are delicately winged and dangle on wiry stems, usually too low to the ground or close in among the foliage to be seen by the casual observer. New leaves start out bronze, expand to green, and show bronze in fall and winter. Plants spread at a slow to moderate pace. This evergreen complements winter-interest shade plants, such as coral bells and foam flower. The subtle two-tone foliage echoes pink-flowered bleeding heart, cardinal flower, fringe-cup, lungwort, and geranium. Plants are especially elegant combined with large blue-leaved hostas.
Care: Barrenwort tolerates drought, dense shade, and competition from tree roots. It is basically pest-free, but root weevils are sometimes a problem. Plants are resistant to rabbits and browsing deer. Cut down the previous year's foliage in late fall or late winter so that next year's flowers are more visible. There is no need to deadhead. Division is rarely required. Plants have offsets and are easy to move.
Recommended plants and related species: Longspur barrenwort *(E. grandiflorum)* has the largest flowers. Those of 'Rose Queen' are crimson. 'White Queen' blooms silver-white. 'Pierre's Purple' is taller and has large purple blooms. Foliage of red barrenwort *(E. ×rubrum)* has rosy undertones and margins.

Barrenwort 'Rose Queen'

Red barrenwort

Eremurus × isabellinus
Shelford hybrids foxtail lily

- **Hardiness Zones: 4–8**
- **Heat Zones: 8–1**
- **Light: Full sun**
- **Size: 4–8'H×3'W**
- **Features: Tall spikes with hundreds of yellow flowers**

Shelford Hybrids foxtail lily

Few perennials have the stature of foxtail lily. The plant sends up 4- to 8-foot-tall pointed spikes that are packed with small, ¼- to ¾-inch-wide flowers along its upper half in late spring or early summer. Flowers open from top to bottom, and depending upon species or cultivar, may be white, pink, orange, or yellow. Leaves develop in early spring, surrounding a flower bud, then disappearing by midsummer.
Care: Plant in well-drained soil and in a location protected from winds. Plants grow well where summers are hot and dry; spring and fall are rainy. Plant carefully; roots are brittle and will rot if damaged. Set in holes so crowns are 1½ inches below grade. Lift and divide in summer, after leaves are gone, by carefully untangling roots.
Recommended plants and related species: Cultivars include 3- to 6-foot-tall, orange-red 'Cleopatra', and 5- to 6-foot-tall, pink to orange 'Isobel'.

Erigeron
Fleabane

- **Hardiness Zones: 4–7**
- **Heat Zones: 8–4**
- **Light: Full sun**
- **Size: 1–2'H×2'W**
- **Features: Wide range of colors, midsummer to fall**

This dainty North American native looks like an aster but is even easier to grow. And it blooms earlier. Fleabane is a carefree plant for the front or middle of a sunny border. Plant in drifts of three or more for color all season long.
Care: Plant 12 to 18 inches apart in well-drained soil. Cut back after flowering to reduce weediness and rejuvenate the foliage. Taller varieties may require staking. Divide every three years.
Recommended plants and related species: There are many cultivars of hybrid orgin as well as distinct species. Top cultivars include 'Azure Beauty' (30 inches tall, semidouble, lavender-blue flowers); 'Rosa Triumph' (24 inches tall, clear pink double flowers); 'Dimity' (12 inches tall, pink blooms); and 'Foerster's Liebling' (16 inches tall, deep pink flowers). Species include *E. karvinskianus,* a dwarf trailing plant that bears masses of white-to-pink flowers throughout the summer. It is hardy in Zones 8 to 9 but reseeds itself freely in colder climates so comes back each year.

Fleabane and stonecrop

Eryngium amethystinum
Amethyst sea holly

- **Hardiness Zones: 2–8**
- **Heat Zones: 8–4**
- **Light: Full sun**
- **Size: 2'H×2'W**
- **Features: Profuse, steely blue flowers, midsummer**

Amethyst sea holly

Stiff and prickly, this easy-care plant creates a striking effect in a garden. Its handsome form provides interesting contrast in the second tier of a border, combined with artemisias or yellow yarrows. Of the several *Eryngium* species, amethyst sea holly is the most cold hardy and the most common.
Care: Plant amethyst sea holly in full sun in well-drained soil. Dry, sandy soils are ideal. Sow seeds in spring or set out nursery plants 15 to 18 inches apart. The plant's taproot makes it difficult to move or divide. Plants seldom need staking. Tolerance to salt spray makes amethyst sea holly a good candidate for a seaside garden.
Recommended plants and related species: Alpine sea holly, *E. alpinum,* grows about 2 feet tall and is hardy in Zones 4 to 8. The cultivar 'Blue Star' has large lavender-blue flowers that resemble fireworks. *E. ×oliverianum* is 3 feet tall with pale blue flowers and deeply cut foliage. Flat sea holly, *E. planum* 'Blue Cap', has intense blue flowers.

Eupatorium coelestinum
Hardy ageratum

- Hardiness Zones: 6–10
- Heat Zones: 9–1
- Light: Full sun to shade
- Size: 2–3'H×3'W
- Features: Powder blue flowers, late summer to fall

Hardy ageratum

Like all eupatoriums, hardy ageratum is prized for its late-season blooms. Its feathery blue flowers open from late summer into fall. Flowers are only about ½ inch wide, but so many are clustered together that the effect is quite impressive. Leaves are roughly triangular, about 3 inches long. Plants grow in mounds and may be much wider than tall. They spread by shallow stolons below the soil's surface. Be wary, though, as plants can grow and spread fast, treading the line between friend and foe. Annual ageratum, also known as floss flower, and hardy ageratum are so similar they can be difficult to distinguish. You can check two features: First, leaves of hardy ageratum have little or no odor when crushed, while annual ageratum has a fragrance. Second, annual ageratum does not spread by stolons.

Care: Plant in well-drained, moist soil. Divide plants every four to five years by digging up offsets and replanting. Pinch plants to keep them compact and prevent floppiness. Deadhead to reduce self-seeding, and pull wandering plants annually to keep them in check; new plants can grow from small sections of root.

Recommended plants and related species: 'Album' has white flowers. A much larger relative, spotted joe-pye weed, *E. maculatum*, reaches nearly 7 feet tall and produces mauve flowers in late summer. Cultivars include 'Atropurpureum' (reddish-purple stems); 'Gateway' (compact, bronze stems; huge, light-color blooms); and 'Little Joe', is 4 feet tall. All are hardy to Zone 3.

Joe-pye weed and feather reed grass

Euphorbia polychroma
Cushion spurge

- Hardiness Zones: 4–7
- Heat Zones: Varies by species
- Light: Full to half sun
- Size: 12–20"H×24"W
- Features: Chartreuse bracts, early to midspring

Cushion spurge

Cushion spurge is a colorful addition to gardens with its clusters of tiny flowers backed by showy, long-lasting chartreuse bracts on top of each stem. It is a strongly mounded, clump-forming plant, with a slow- to moderate-growth rate.

Care: Plant in any well-drained soil. Cushion spurge tolerates heat, wind, and alkaline soil, but does not grow well where summer humidity is high. Deadhead to avoid self-sowing; plants can become weedy in moist soils. Divide plants every five to six years to reduce crowding; they have offsets. Plants are resistant to rabbits, woodchucks, and deer.

Recommended plants and related species: 'Purpurea' has a purple cast to the foliage. Griffith's spurge *(E. griffithii)* is strongly columnar and 30 inches tall. Cultivars include 'Fireglow' (flowers resemble glowing, then fading embers); 'Dixter' (flowers are red, fading to orange); and 'First Blush' (has yellow flowers and green-white-pink variegation, until the green remains and the pink fades).

Festuca glauca
(F. ovina glauca)
Blue fescue

- Hardiness Zones: 4–8
- Heat Zones: 7–1
- Light: Full sun to shade
- Size: 6–10"H×6–10"W
- Features: Ornamental grass with silvery blue foliage

Blue fescue 'Elijah Blue'

This cousin of one of the most popular lawn grasses, red fescue *(F. rubra)*, shows the family resemblence in its needlelike leaves. But instead of the spreading bright green grass that grows in lawns, blue fescue grows as a mound and has blue- to silver-green leaves. Plants make a compact border, and their color is useful in many situations for the contrast it provides.

Care: Plant in any well-drained soil, spacing clumps about 8 inches apart. Plants are drought tolerant. Shear off summertime flower spikes after they brown to keep plants neat. Divide plants every other year to prolong the plants' life. In heavy clay soils the plants may be short-lived.

Recommended plants and related species: Three of the best of the cultivars include 'Blue Silver' (silver-leaved); 'Elijah Blue' (powder blue leaves); and 'Solling' (silver-gray foliage, non-flowering).

Filipendula vulgaris
Dropwort

- Hardiness Zones: 3–8
- Heat Zones: 9–1
- Light: Sun to shade
- Size: 1–7'H×1–3'W
- Features: Creamy flowers from late spring to early summer

The pinkish flower buds of dropwort open to creamy white flowers. They are densely clustered at the tips of tall, nearly leafless stems. The flower stalks rise 3 feet above mounded foliage. Plants develop into a clump form.

Care: Dropwort tolerates almost any garden soil but prefers one that is rich in organic matter. It takes heat, if given partial shade and constant moisture, and dry soil where air is cool. It also takes high humidity, wind, and alkaline soil. Cut plants back in early spring. Deadhead to prolong bloom and to reduce self-sowing. Divide every five to six years in spring or fall; plants have offsets and are easy to move.

Recommended plants and related species: Meadowsweet *(F. ulmaria)* produces white flowers in early summer. The shade-tolerant plants grow 3 to 5 feet tall. Queen-of-the-prairie *(F. rubra)* is 3 to 7 feet tall, and has pink cotton-candy blooms in early to midsummer. Varieties include 'Flore Pleno' (double flowers); 'Kahome' (dwarf, pink); and 'Venusta' (deep pink).

Dropwort

Gaillardia aristata
(G. grandiflora)
Blanket flower

- Hardiness Zones: 3–9
- Heat Zones: 12–1
- Light: Full sun
- Size: 2'H×2'W
- Features: Yellow and red daisies, summer to early fall

Blanket flower 'Arizona Sun'

Blanket flowers are loosely upright perennials with coarse blue-gray foliage at the base of the plant. They produce large daisies with yellow-marked red petals and warm red-brown centers. Plants are clump forming; short, running roots spread quickly.

Care: Plant in well-drained, moist soil. Blanket flower blooms continuously from summer into fall, even without deadheading, though faded blossoms detract from blooming flowers and make the plant appear ragged. Deadhead for neatness, or allow some seed to develop for new plants. Use grow-through supports or crutches to prevent floppiness.

Recommended plants and related species: 'Arizona Sun' (12 inches tall, orange-red flowers with yellow tips); 'Baby Cole' (10 inches tall, wide red zone); 'Burgundy' (24 inches tall, red); 'Goblin' (9 to 15 inches tall, with mostly red-tipped petals); and 'Fanfare' (red and yellow petals are tubular with a scarlet lining, flaring at their tips).

Galium odoratum (Asperula odorata)
Sweet woodruff

- ◾ **Hardiness Zones: 4–8**
- ◾ **Heat Zones: 8–3**
- ◾ **Light: Half sun to dense shade**
- ◾ **Size: 6–12"H×6–12"W**
- ◾ **Features: Handsome leaves all season, and tiny white flowers in spring**

Sweet woodruff

When sweet woodruff's bright green leaves are crushed, they emit a fragrance similar to freshly mown hay. The divided, rough-edged leaves are arranged in whorls along the stem. The leaves are evergreen and change from bright green in summer to light brown in winter. Tiny, star-shape white or yellow flowers appear in clusters. Use sweet woodruff as an underplanting for thick shrubs; in any shaded spot; or interspersed with lilies and other perennials.

Care: Plant in well-drained, good-quality, slightly acid soil. Space sweet woodruff plants 12 inches apart. They grow best in part sun or shade. Where summers are cool, sweet woodruff tolerates sun. It can be invasive. Plants spread by underground runners, and once established, they spread quickly. Pull runners that creep outside the boundaries you've allotted for them. Propagate sweet woodruff by division.

Gaura lindheimeri
White gaura

- ◾ **Hardiness Zones: 5–9**
- ◾ **Heat Zones: 9–2**
- ◾ **Light: Full to half sun**
- ◾ **Size: 18–60"H×12–36"W**
- ◾ **Features: White flowers, midsummer into fall**

Gaura's dainty flowers dance on wiry stems. Buds are pink, and flowers are white, turning pink with age. Plants continuously produce new flowers without deadheading. In areas with warm springs, plants bloom early. They form an airy column 3 to 5 feet tall, sometimes taller in warm areas. They are clump forming and fast growing.

Care: Plant in well-drained soil that has been amended with organic matter. Gaura tolerates drought, heat, humidity, and wind but not wet soil. Its blooms may fall off in midsummer if nights are hot. Deadhead occasionally to keep new flower stalks developing. Cut plants back in spring, not fall, after new leaves emerge.

Recommended plants and related species: 'Pink Cloud' has pale pink flowers. 'Crimson Butterfly' has reddish foliage and stems; it grows 1½ to 2 feet. 'Whirling Butterflies' is white; it reaches 1½ to 2 feet; 'Siskiyou Pink' is deep pink and 1½ to 2 feet tall.

Gaura 'Pink Cloud'

Geranium sanguineum
Bloody cranesbill

- ◾ **Hardiness Zones: 3–8**
- ◾ **Heat Zones: 12–2**
- ◾ **Light: Full to half sun**
- ◾ **Size: 1–2'H×2'W**
- ◾ **Features: Red-violet, pink, or white flowers, mid- to late spring**

Bloody cranesbill

Bloody cranesbill is the classic perennial geranium for care-free color in the border. It shows off best in small gardens or at close range. It is a long-lived, clump-forming perennial. One-inch-wide blooms stud the plant from mid- to late spring and sporadically all summer. The growth rate is moderate to fast.

Care: Plant in any well-drained, moist soil in a location that receives full sun or light shade. Space plants 15 inches apart. Shear plants after they bloom for fresh foliage. In early spring cut back hard if plants had leaf spot the previous year. Divide plants every five to six years to renew vigor; they have running roots and are easy to move. Bloody cranesbill is pest-free, but leaf spot can be a problem. Remove all infected foliage and destroy it.

Recommended plants and related species: 'Max Frei' has purple-pink blooms on compact plants. 'Album' has white blooms. The variety Lancastriense tolerates heat and cold better than others.

Geranium hybrids
Geranium

- **Hardiness Zones: 4–7**
- **Heat Zones: 7–1**
- **Light: Half sun**
- **Size: 10–24"H×24–60"W**
- **Features: Pink or blue flowers, spring through fall**

Hybrid geranium 'Rozanne'

During the past several years, gardeners in North America have discovered the great beauty and variety of geraniums—flowers that have long been popular in England. Because of the generally more-rigorous climate here, not all of the transplants did well at first. Now, several have distinguished themselves as stalwart perennials on this continent.

Care: Plant in rich, moist, well-drained soil, the latter being key to vigorous growth. Full sun, perhaps with afternoon shade, is preferred in cool areas, but plant in shade if your summers are hot and long. Space plants 18 inches apart. In early spring cut back hard if desired or if plants had leaf spot the previous year. Propagate by division, every two to three years or as needed.

Recommended plants and related species: Of the many species and cultivars of geraniums the following intergeneric hybrids are among the most popular today.

Showy geranium, *G. ×magnificum*, produces dark blue flowers and thick, deeply cut leaves. Flowers are held high above leaves.

'Ann Folkard' is delightful, especially when displaying its ability to climb into and over shrubs and other plants. Its 1½-inch-diameter flowers are purple magenta with a prominent black center and veins.

'Anne Thomson' has golden leaves and violet flowers, but perhaps most important, it has excellent heat tolerance. It blooms from spring until midsummer in Zone 7.

'Philippe Vapelle' produces a tight clump of 3-inch-wide leaves with scalloped edges. Flowers are violet blue with darker veins.

'Pink Spice' develops into a 10-inch-tall mound of foliage and 1-inch-diameter pink flowers. It has a long bloom season.

'Rozanne' is heat tolerant, producing blue flowers above a spreading clump of leaves from spring until fall. Many experts consider this the best hybrid geranium available.

'Silver Sugar Plum' ('Frances Grate') grows only 18 inches tall but sprawls to 5 feet wide or more. Leaves are gray-green on top but silvery underneath. Lilac-mauve flowers are 1 inch in diameter. This plant can reseed itself, sometimes annoyingly so.

The flowers of 'Spinners' are purple-blue with dark pink veins and a pale center, and they bloom from spring through fall.

Showy geranium

Geum
Geum

- **Hardiness Zones: 4–7**
- **Heat Zones: 9–3**
- **Light: Full sun or afternoon shade**
- **Size: 1–2'H×1–2'W**
- **Features: Red, orange, or yellow flowers, late spring through summer**

Geum 'Princess Juliana'

Geum makes a showy display of eye-catching colors on attractive dark green foliage. It is appealing at the front of the border, backed by the cool blues of delphinium or bellflower.

Care: Plant in well-drained, humus-rich soil, in a location that receives full sun in cool regions. Where summers are hot, afternoon shade is mandatory. Space plants 12 to 18 inches apart. During the growing season, water abundantly. Deadhead to prolong bloom. Geum has no serious pests or diseases if plants are sited correctly. You can propagate by division, though it's rarely needed.

Recommended plants and related species: 'Borisii' and 'Werner Arends' are cultivars of *G. coccineum*. The former has yellow flowers and the latter's flowers are semidouble orange-red. 'Mrs. Bradshaw Improved', a cultivar of *G. chiloense,* has brick-red, semidouble flowers. It grows 1 to 2 feet tall. 'Princess Juliana' has soft-yellow, double blooms.

Gunnera manicata
Gunnera

- Hardiness Zones: 7–10
- Heat Zones: 8–2
- Light: Sun or shade
- Size: 7'H×8'W
- Features: Gigantic coarse-texture, umbrella-shape leaves

Gunnera

Gunnera's coarse mounds of enormous 4-foot-wide, umbrella-shape leaves grow to a colossal 6 to 8 feet tall. Gunnera is not widely adapted; only a few North American gardeners can grow it successfully. But if you're among the fortunate few in a mild-winter, cool-summer climate, don't miss the opportunity. Grow it poolside or as an accent.
Care: Grow gunnera in sun or partial shade in moist or wet, fertile soil. If not provided with adequate moisture, gunnera leaves turn brown and dry up. Allow 8 feet between plants. Keep soil moist and fertilize two to three times. Gunnera thrives in cool climates, where temperatures seldom top 80°F.
Recommended plants and related species: Spreading *G. magellanica* is a mat-forming plant with 2-inch-wide, dark-green kidney-shape leaves that serves well as a groundcover. *G. tinctoria* is slightly smaller than *G. manicata*, at 6 feet tall, and has reddish flowers hidden among the foliage.

Gypsophila paniculata
Baby's breath

- Hardiness Zones: 3–7
- Heat Zones: 9–3
- Light: Full sun
- Size: 2–3'H×3'W
- Features: Billows of white flowers, summer

Baby's breath, a ubiquitous component of fresh and dried floral arrangements, is a charming, easy-to-grow addition to the home landscape. Airy and delicate, it makes a delightful backdrop for other summer-blooming perennials and is a perfect complement for foxglove or lilies. It is a definite must for the cut-flower garden.
Care: Plant baby's breath in sandy, well-drained, alkaline soil. Adjust pH by adding limestone if soil is acidic. Space plants 3 feet apart. Support the plants with grow-through stakes. Division is not recommended.
Recommended plants and related species: 'Bristol Fairy' has double white flowers and grows 2 to 3 feet tall. 'Fairy Perfect' has large double white flowers. 'Flamingo' is 3 to 4 feet tall and bears double pink flowers. Creeping baby's breath *(G. repens)* is a wonderful plant for the front border. It reaches only 6 to 12 inches tall and has white to lilac flowers. Less hardy 'Rosea' is 8 inches tall with pale pink flowers.

Baby's breath

Hakonechloa macra 'All Gold'
Golden hakone grass

- Hardiness Zones: 4–8
- Heat Zones: 9–4
- Light: Half sun to shade
- Size: 1–2'H×2–3'W
- Features: Colorful, leafy accent

Golden hakone grass

This ornamental grass is slow to establish but worth the wait, eventually forming a dense mass. Its bright yellow markings light up shady gardens and are smashing with hostas, especially ones with yellow-edge, dark green leaves. Hakone grass develops a pinkish-red to bronze color in fall. Plants are clump forming and do not bloom.
Care: Plant in rich, moist, well-drained, acidic soil, and in a location that receives filtered light. Space plants 12 to 15 inches apart. Trim back faded foliage in early spring to neaten appearance. Avoid heat and drought.
Recommended plants and related species: 'Aureola' has yellow and green stripes; 'Albo-Marginata' has green and white stripes.

Helenium autumnale
Helenium

- **Hardiness Zones: 3–8**
- **Heat Zones: 8–1**
- **Light: Full sun**
- **Size: 3–5'H×3'W**
- **Features: Hot-colored blooms, late summer**

Helenium 'Red and Gold'

Helenium is a sturdy, adaptable plant that is native to the wet meadows of eastern North America. It grows 3 to 5 feet tall, depending on moisture availability and variety. Plants bloom for 8 to 10 weeks. This perennial lends the border a late-summer color boost and combines well with asters or ornamental grasses.

Care: Plant in moist and rich soil for most vigorous growth. Space plants 18 to 24 inches apart. Stake taller varieties. Cut back after flowering to keep disease and insects at bay. Divide plants when crowded, usually every other year. Fertilize sparingly.

Recommended plants and related species: Look for compact, less rangy varieties. Favorites include 'Brilliant' (many bronze flowers); 'Moerheim Beauty' (rusty red, changing to orange and gold, 3- to 4-foot plants); 'Red and Gold', (red and gold flowers on 3- to 4-foot plants); and 'Wyndley' (2 to 3 feet tall, coppery brown flowers).

Helianthus decapetalus (H. multiflorus)
Thinleaf sunflower

- **Hardiness Zones: 4–8**
- **Heat Zones: 9–1**
- **Light: Half to full sun**
- **Size: 3–6'H×3–4'W**
- **Features: Yellow flowers in late summer to fall**

Thinleaf sunflower is a dependable back-of-the-border plant. It is valued for its late-season effect and statuesque presence. The bright, 3-inch-wide flowers may be single or double. Plants form a sturdy column that is half as wide as it is tall, gradually becoming wider. The growth rate is moderate to fast.

Care: Perennial sunflower tolerates half sun, heavy clay, and a wide pH range. Pinch the plant several times from midspring to early summer to restrict height. Deadhead to prolong bloom. Double-flowered forms are seedless. Taller varieties may need staking with individual braces or long crutches. Maintain constant moisture and divide every three years in fall or spring to facilitate air circulation through the clump.

Recommended plants and related species: 'Flore-pleno' has double flowers and grows 5 feet tall. 'Capenoch Star' is light yellow and reaches 4 feet tall.

Thinleaf sunflower 'Flore-pleno'

Helictotrichon sempervirens
Blue oat grass

- **Hardiness Zones: 3–7**
- **Heat Zones: 9–1**
- **Light: Full sun**
- **Size: 30"H×30"W**
- **Features: Fine-texture, steely blue ornamental grass**

Blue oat grass

Blue oat grass resembles blue fescue but forms substantially larger clumps. It has attractive foliage and a beautiful-but-sporadic, spiky form. Oatlike flowers on arching stems start off brownish and turn a golden wheat hue in fall. Grow blue oat grass as a specimen or in mass plantings. An excellent partner for coral bells, the plant has blue-gray foliage that works well in gardens needing a color cool-down.

Care: Plant in well-drained , dry soil with a neutral or nearly neutral pH. Space plants 2 to 3 feet apart. In late winter, comb or rake out brown foliage; divide them every three years. Plants are prone to fungal attack in humid climates. Winter mulch is recommended in areas colder than Zone 5.

Recommended plants and related species: 'Sapphire Fountain' has bluer leaves than the species and is more weather tolerant.

Heliopsis helianthoides var. *scabra*
False sunflower

- **Hardiness Zones: 3–8**
- **Heat Zones: 9–1**
- **Light: Full sun**
- **Size: 3–6'H×2–4'W**
- **Features: Yellow flowers early to late summer**

False sunflower

Bright color, large 3-inch flowers, and long bloom time make false sunflower indispensable in informal borders. Plants are clump-forming and fast-growing. Use as a backdrop or partner for shorter, finer-textured mounded perennials, such as lavender, catmint, Chinese peony, and meadow sage.

Care: False sunflower tolerates drought, half sun, a wide pH range, and clay soil. Only wet or poorly drained soil inhibits it. False sunflower needs midday shade in hot regions. Cut plants back in late fall or early spring. Plants self-sow; seedlings will be variable and most likely inferior to the original plant. Divide clumps every two to three years to maintain vigor and full bloom.

Recommended plants and related species: 'Prairie Sunset' has purple stems that reach 6 feet tall, then produce masses of 2-inch gold-orange flowers. 'Summer Sun', with soft yellow, double flower reaches 3 to 5 feet tall.

Helleborus orientalis (*H. × hybridus*)
Lenten rose

- **Hardiness Zones: 4–9**
- **Heat Zones: 8–1**
- **Light: Half sun to shade**
- **Size: 12–18"H×18–30"W**
- **Features: Cream, green, purple, or pink flowers, late winter to early spring**

An early delight for winter-weary gardeners, Lenten rose is one of the finest perennials in cultivation. Its saucer-shape flowers are 2 to 3 inches wide in nodding or out-facing clusters. Blooms may be multihued; for example, pink petals may be flushed with purple or green. Buds are borne upward over several days as stems elongate. These evergreen, clump-forming plants have lustrous foliage. Lenten rose complements perennials with ferny, pale foliage or columnar shapes, such as astilbe, Kamchatka bugbane, bleeding heart, jacob's ladder, and cardinal flower.

Care: Provide a shady site with moist, well-drained soil. Plants do not grow well in wet or poorly drained soil, windy areas, or warm spring weather. They will tolerate dry and alkaline soils. Lenten rose can thrive in full sun if the climate is cool and plants have ample water during winter. Fertilize as new foliage

Lenten rose

emerges. Plants do not require deadheading, but they may self-sow. The resulting seedlings are often pleasing. Transplant them before the expanding foliage shades them out. Prune dead leaves in late winter to make way for new growth and flowers. Plants seldom need division once established. But when it is

Lenten rose 'Pink Lady'

necessary, divide plants in spring so plants have time to reestablish before winter. They may not bloom the year after dividing. In Zones 4 to 5, provide extra protection if snow cover is not reliable. Pests include slugs, snails, and root weevils. Leaf spot can occur if soil is quite heavy or acid. Remove infected foliage and apply fungicide if sanitary measures do not help. Because plants are toxic, deer and rabbits don't browse them, but neither should children.

Recommended plants and related species: Lenten rose is usually available in mixed but unidentified colors. 'Brandywine' is a new series that produces dark red, spotted pink, apricot, and often-double yellow flowers. 'Pink Lady' flowers are light pink except for the contrasting purple spots. 'Double Vision' is deep pink, light pink, purple, red, and white. 'Dusk' and 'Pluto' have dark purple blooms. 'Cosmos' is white. 'Royal Heritage' has a mix of colors from white to red.

Hemerocallis
Daylily

- **Hardiness Zones: 3–9**
- **Heat Zones: 12–1**
- **Light: Full sun to shade**
- **Size: 1–3'H×2–3'W**
- **Features: Flowers in white, yellow, orange, red, or purple and all shades in between**

Daylily flowers may be plain or ruffled, striped or bicolored, single or double. Plant heights range from 12-inch minis to 36-inch giants. Some varieties are evergreen; these do best in southern regions. Flowers may skim the top of the foliage or rise several feet. Most plants are clump-forming with a moderate growth rate. Some spread quickly. Peak bloom time is midsummer, but some cultivars bloom in late spring, others in early, mid-, or late summer. Repeat bloomers have several flushes each year. A few superstars bloom continuously from late spring to fall frost. Showy but easy, daylilies blend beautifully with most perennials.

Care: Daylilies withstand heat, drought, shade, salt, foot traffic, flooding, wind, and competition from tree roots. Grow them in full or half sun. They do best in humus-rich, well-drained, and consistently moist soil. Plant daylilies anytime during the growing season, even when plants

A mass planting of 'Hyperion' daylily makes a dramatic summer show.

are in bloom. Leave approximately 1½ to 3 feet between plants, depending on the variety. Fertilize regularly but not heavily. Snap off spent flowers at their base. Divide every three to five years, when the number of blossoms declines.

Slugs, snails, and late-spring frost damage make plants vulnerable to disease. Plants attract rabbits, woodchucks, and deer.

Recommended plants and related species: Here is a sampler of cultivars. Rebloomers: 'Stella de Oro', golden yellow blooms, spring to frost; 'Pardon Me', vigorous, bright red with a yellow

throat; 'Happy Returns', lemon yellow flowers, reblooms in all climates, hot or cold. Extended, day-long bloom (flowers last 16 hours or more): 'Daring Dilemma', creamy pink. Late spring to early summer bloom: 'Siloam Purple Plum' and 'Lullaby Baby', ice pink with green throat. Early summer: 'Astolat' and 'Coral'. Mid- to late summer: 'Cherry Cheeks', 'August Flame', and 'September Gold'. Summer to fall bloom: 'Autumn Minaret'. Fragrant flowers: 'Hyperion', lemon yellow. Miniature (small flowers on full-size plants): 'Golden Chimes'.

'Stella de Oro' daylily

'Pardon Me' daylily

'Cherry Cheeks' daylily

Heuchera sanguinea
Coral bells

- **Hardiness Zones: 3–8**
- **Heat Zones: 8–2**
- **Light: Shade to full sun**
- **Size: 6–24"H×6–12"W**
- **Features: Attractive leaves and red, pink, or white flowers, late spring**

Coral bells 'Obsidian'

Loved for its tiny, wiry-stemmed blooms, coral bells is available with striking foliage. Leaves may be ruffled, lobed, or marbled with contrasting veins. The plants grow in clumps and work well in beds at the front of a border.
Care: Plant in well-drained soil that is rich in organic matter. Water regularly. Plants can compete with tree roots if topdressed with 1 to 2 inches of compost every fall. Deadhead to prolong bloom. In winter, cover plants with loose mulch, such as evergreen boughs, to prevent frost heaving. Cut away old foliage in early spring.
Recommended plants and related species: Varieties with green foliage include: 'Chatterbox' (large pink flowers) and 'Firebird' (deep red flowers). Purple-leaf coral bells include 'Chocolate Ruffles' (deep maroon leaves); 'Lime Rickey' (chartreuse leaves have ruffled margins); 'Peach Flambé' (red-orange new growth); and 'Obsidian' (leaves are ruby red). These hybrids are hardy in Zones 4 to 9.

×*Heucherella*
Foamy bells

- **Hardiness Zones: 4–9**
- **Heat Zones: 8–2**
- **Light: Partial shade**
- **Size: 4–5"H×12"W**
- **Features: Plumes of flowers in spring and attractive leaves all season**

These are intergeneric hybrids (two different genera) between coral bells *(Heuchera,* at left) and foam flower *(Tiarella,* page 118), combining characteristics of both parents. Generally, they have the flowers of coral bells and the leaves of foam flower. All types excel in shaded rock gardens or as woodland groundcovers. Cultivars differ primarily in leaf colors and markings, while all produce plumes of small flowers that are light to dark pink.
Care: Plants require well-drained soils that are rich in organic matter. While cutting back leaves in fall is not recommended, remove any that are dead or nearly so in early spring.
Recommended plants and related species: 'Stoplight' has lime green leaves with a crimson center; 'Day Glow Pink' has bright green leaves marked with purple veins; 'Quicksilver' has bronze veins in metallic silver leaves; 'Rosemary Bloom' has rich green leaves and forms a clump that reaches 18 to 24 inches tall.

Foamy bells 'Day Glow Pink'

Hibiscus moscheutos
Hardy hibiscus

- **Hardiness Zones: 5–10**
- **Heat Zones: 10–1**
- **Light: Full sun**
- **Size: 20–60"H×36"W**
- **Features: Pink, red, and white flowers, mid- to late summer**

Hardy hibiscus

Hardy hisbiscus has large maple-shape leaves and huge dark-eye flowers that reach 8 to 12 inches wide. It contrasts handsomely with vertical plants and perennials with finer texture or smaller flowers, such as Japanese water iris, liatris, cardinal flower, and culver's root.
Care: Plants need rich soil and plenty of heat to bloom well. Native to marshlands, they don't tolerate drought. Divide every decade or so, using a saw to cut through woody roots. Plants are easy to start from seed; seedlings bloom their first year. Cut plants back in late fall or early spring.
Recommended plants and related species: 'Disco Belle' has 9-inch pink, red, or white flowers on 20- to 30-inch-tall plants. 'Kopper King' has coppery red maplelike leaves. 'Southern Belle' has 10- to 12-inch red, pink, or white blooms on plants 3 to 4 feet tall. Scarlet rose mallow *(H. coccineus)* grows 6 to 8 feet tall, half as wide, and has large red funnel-shape flowers (Zones 6 to 9). It requires moist soil.

Hosta
Hosta

- Hardiness Zones: 3–8
- Heat Zones: 8–1
- Light: Half sun to shade
- Size: 6–36"H×6–30"W
- Features: Large, variously colored leaves

'Sum and Substance' hosta

Hostas have showy gold, blue, green, or variegated leaves that may be puckered, ruffled, or quilted, and vary from oval to oblong, narrow to wide. Lilac or white bell-shape flowers hang from stalks that rise above the mound of foliage in midsummer. For most cultivars, the flowers are not the attraction.

Care: Plant hostas in well-drained soil that has a neutral to slightly acidic pH. Hostas tolerate sun if temperatures are cool and water plentiful. Yellow-leaf cultivars are more likely to do well in sun than blue-leaf ones. Alkaline soil is acceptable, but plants do not tolerate drought. Fertilize plants regularly. Divide them every seven to eight years; they grow from offsets and are easy to move. In late fall or early spring, cut down plants and topdress with compost. Deadheading depends on the species. Some are weak bloomers with floppy flower stems; cut these off before blooms open. Other species have

'Patriot' hosta

substantial flowers on sturdy stalks. The big, blue-leaf hostas produce more flowers if the season is long and you remove the first blooms before seed sets. Slugs, snails, rabbits, and deer can ruin hosta foliage. If you live where deer browse, hostas are not a good choice. Varieties with thick leaves and quilted surfaces are more resistant to slugs. Under trees that host heavy insect populations, sooty mold may blemish leaves. Rinse foliage regularly, and plant smooth-leaf hostas, which self-clean better than quilted types.

Recommended plants and related species: There are many hosta cultivars, ranging in size from 8-inch dwarf specimens, such as *H. venusta,* to 3-feet-tall giants, such as 'Sum and Substance'. Here are some others to consider:

Blue-leaf siebold hostas *(H. sieboldiana)* include 'Elegans', with large leaves in amber fall color, and 'Frances Williams', with large leaves irregularly edged in creamy yellow. 'Great Expectations' has blue edges around a leaf center streaked cream, gold, and green.

H. nigrescens has lance-shape gray-green foliage. Varieties include 'Krossa Regal', which forms an upright, vase-shape clump. Its flower stalks rise 3 to 6 feet tall.

H. nakaiana varieties include 'Golden Tiara', which has small, heart-shape leaves edged in gold.

The dense, heavy blooming clumps are 8 to 12 inches tall, with slightly taller purple flowers.

Blue hosta *(H. ventricosa)* has large, smooth, shiny foliage and dark purple flowers. 'Aureo-marginata' has wide, creamy white irregular edges on the leaves.

'Krossa Regal' hosta

The scented white blooms of fragrant hosta *(H. plantaginea)* resemble flaring trumpets. Plants bloom in late summer, after most other hostas have finished flowering. They reach 24 inches tall when blooming and 24 inches wide. The light green foliage is more prone to slug and snail damage than others.

Hybrids include 'Sugar and Cream', with fragrant, pale lilac flowers and quilted, slug-resistant foliage in Zones 4 to 9.

'Golden Tiara' hosta

Iberis sempervirens
Evergreen candytuft

- Hardiness Zones: 3–9
- Heat Zones: 9–1
- Light: Full to half sun
- Size: 6–12"H×12–18"W
- Features: Bright white flowers, early- to midspring

Evergreen candytuft

In spring, evergreen candytuft forms a carpet of white blooms over a mat of fine-texture, dark evergreen foliage. It is particularly attractive trailing over a stone wall. Plants grow at a moderate pace. Evergreen candytuft complements mounded or vertical plants with coarse texture, and species with winter interest, such as coral bells, iris, and thrift. It blooms at the same time as early blooming columbines.

Care: Plant in well-drained soil that is amended with organic matter. Cut back or shear by one-half after bloom to promote dense growth and to keep plants compact. Divide evergreen candytuft every four to five years in spring or fall, and add organic matter when replanting. If snow cover is not reliable in cold regions, foliage will die back; prune out any damage in spring.

Recommended plants and related species: 'Alexander's White' has especially dense foliage and is free-flowering.

Imperata cylindrica 'Red Baron'
Japanese blood grass

- Hardiness Zones: 5–9
- Heat Zones: 9–3
- Light: Full sun
- Size: 12–18"H×24"W
- Features: Brilliant red foliage

Japanese blood grass grows into 12- to 18-inch-tall upright clumps. In cooler climates, it gets redder as the season progresses. It is not a good choice for hot, dry areas; the farther south this grass is grown, the less its red color is evident. Mass it with silver-gray plants, such as lamb's-ears, or grow it in containers with other perennials. In fall, its beautiful red color, backlit by the sun, is unforgettable.

Care: Plant in moist, well-drained soil in a location that receives full sun (so plants develop best color). Space plants 12 to 15 inches apart. The straight species can be invasive. And in some areas, especially warm climates, the sale and distribution of Japanese blood grass is prohibited. Green forms are especially problematic. Occasionally 'Red Baron' reverts to its green-leaf parent, and these much more vigorous shoots should be eliminated to prevent their spreading.

Japanese blood grass

Inula ensifolia
Swordleaf inula

- Hardiness Zones: 4–8
- Heat Zones: Not rated
- Light: Full sun
- Size: 1–2'H×2'W
- Features: Long-lasting, narrow-petal yellow flowers, early summer

Swordleaf inula

The plants grow in a dense mound, spreading by short, shallow rhizomes at a moderate growth rate. The fine-textured sword-leaf inula combines with coarse vase-shape and columnar plants, such as butterfly weed, yarrow, clustered bellflower, meadow sage, blue oat grass, liatris, thinleaf sunflower, and long-leaf speedwell.

Care: Plant in well-drained soil that has plenty of organic matter. Plants tolerate wind but not a combination of high heat and humidity, or wet, poorly drained soil. Shear plants after flowering for repeat bloom. In early spring, cut them to the ground. Divide plants every four to five years in spring or fall; they have offsets and are easy to move. Add organic matter to the soil when replanting. Plants are basically pest free.

Recommended plants and related species: 'Compacta' grows less than a foot tall and 12 to 18 inches wide. It attracts butterflies.

Iris cristata
Crested iris

- **Hardiness Zones: 3–8**
- **Heat Zones: Not rated**
- **Light: Sun to dense shade**
- **Size: 6–12"H×12"W**
- **Features: Pale lilac-blue flowers, spring**

Crested iris

This lovely, lightly fragrant iris naturalizes well and is a native of the Southeast. Its bright green 4- to 6-inch leaves emerge from a rhizome and spread in fan-shape sprays. One to two pale blue blossoms are produced on each 2- to 3-inch-tall stem. The handsome foliage grows low to the ground, so crested iris works well as a groundcover too. Pair it with bleeding heart or columbine.
Care: Plant rhizomes or container-grown plants in well-drained soil in spring. Crested iris will grow in less-favorable soil conditions with regular watering. Space plants 15 inches apart in partial sun to deep shade or in a site with morning sun. Divide in fall if desired.
Recommended plants and related species: 'Alba' is a handsome white-flowered variety with contrasting yellow crests that is less vigorous than the species (and also not as common). 'Powder Blue Giant' grows 12 inches high and has 3-inch light blue-purple flowers with golden crests and darker blue accents.

Iris douglasiana
Douglas iris

- **Hardiness Zones: 8–10**
- **Heat Zones: Not rated**
- **Light: Sun or light shade**
- **Size: 1–3'H×1–2'W**
- **Features: Native iris produces flowers in a broad range of colors, in late winter and early spring**

These long-lived, mostly evergreen perennials are native to the valleys and mountains of the Pacific coast. In autumn, they produce almost grasslike leaves in a fanlike arrangement from thin rhizomes. Blossoms appear in late winter or early spring, each stalk bearing one to three flowers that open in sequence.
Care: Plant in any soil that is well-drained, and in either sun or shade. Water modestly, if at all, in summer—moist soil during hot weather is fatal. Plant in fall or early spring. Keep plants neat by snapping off shriveled flowers. Or, allow them to ripen naturally and scatter seeds. Cut, rather than pull on, the occasional dead leaf to avoid damaging the rhizome.
Recommended plants and related species: Hundreds of Pacific Coast Hybrid cultivars have been developed, but few are sold by name. An exception is 'Canyon Snow'. It has white flowers with yellow spots.

Douglas iris 'Canyon Snow'

Iris ensata
Japanese water iris

- **Hardiness Zones: 5–9**
- **Heat Zones: 8–1**
- **Light: Full sun or partial shade**
- **Size: 3–4'H×2–3'W**
- **Features: Cool blues, purples, pinks, and whites, late spring or summer**

Japanese water iris 'High Purple'

Japanese water iris is an excellent eye-catcher for wet areas. Beautiful orchidlike flowers top sturdy 3- to 4-feet-tall stems (up to 6 feet in rich, boggy soils in mild climates).
Care: Plant in rich, acidic soil that is continuously moist. Locations in full sun or partial shade are fine, but partial shade is required in the South. Provide plenty of water when plants are in bloom; conditions can be drier the rest of the year. Although they do well in wet sites, plants must have good drainage over winter. Space plants 18 to 24 inches apart.
Recommended plants and related species: 'High Purple' has deep purple flowers with yellow centers. 'Loyalty' has violet-blue blooms marked with yellow on the falls, or lower petals. Yellow flag iris (*I. pseudacorus*) has beardless yellow flowers on stems 2 to 4 feet tall. It thrives in standing water or very moist soil in Zones 5 to 9. However, it is invasive and is banned in some states. Never plant it near natural waterways.

Iris germanica
Bearded Iris

- **Hardiness Zones: 3–10**
- **Heat Zones: 9–1**
- **Light: Full sun**
- **Size: 6–36"H×18"W**
- **Features: Dramatic blooms in a wide array of colors and color combinations, mid- to late spring**

Named for the Greek goddess of the rainbow, bearded iris comes in almost every color imaginable except true red, and often have contrasting beards. Sizes range from 6-inch dwarfs to plants 3 feet tall or more tall. The shortest varieties bloom earlier in spring than taller types, but all peak by early summer. Plants spread by stout rhizomes on or just under the soil's surface. Combine irises with mounded and finer-texture plants, such as a dwarf cultivar of New England aster, yarrow, golden marguerite, pinks, threadleaf coreopsis, catmint, cushion spurge, sword-leaf inula, perennial flax, and black-eyed susan.

Care: Bearded iris prefers well-drained soil of near-neutral pH but tolerates high pH, alkaline soil. Plants tolerate heat, but fare poorly in wet soil or shade. Tall

'Jane Philips' bearded iris

cultivars require staking in windy locations, where soil is rich, and after transplanting. Use individual braces. Deadhead after plants fade to promote growth of new, clean foliage. Divide plants every four years after they finish flowering until August. Their rhizomes have multiple eyes; plants are easy to move. Iris borers, insects that burrow into and ruin the rhizomes, can be a problem. They start by chewing between the folds of the foliage, eating their way down into the root. Iris soft rot follows their feeding and can devastate a planting. Control borers by removing all old foliage every fall and spring. Divide in early summer, when you can easily destroy borer grubs found in the rhizomes.

Recommended plants and related species: There are hundreds of cultivars that differ primarily by height and flower color. The petals of iris flowers are called standards (upright petals) or falls (lower petals). One useful guide to choosing cultivars is the American Iris Society, at www.irises.org, where you can find a great deal of iris information of all kinds, including top-rated and award-winning cultivars. Here are some recommendations by height:

Tall (27½ inches or more tall): 'Beverly Sills' (coral pink); 'Crystal Glitters' (cream and peach); 'Darkside' (purple); 'Fringe Benefits' (orange); 'Lime Fizz' (lime yellow); 'Lullaby of Spring' (yellow and lavender); 'Oktoberfest' (orange); 'Silver Fizz' (silver-lavender); 'Spinning Wheel' (blue-violet and white); and 'Tomorrow's Child' (pink standards and purple falls).

Intermediate (16 to 27½ inches tall): 'Brown Lasso' (yellow-gold); and 'Pink Bubbles' (pink).

Dwarf (8 to 16 inches tall): 'Jane Philips' (pale blue).

'Tomorrow's Child' bearded iris

'Beverly Sills' bearded iris

Iris sibirica
Siberian iris

- **Hardiness Zones: 3–9**
- **Heat Zones: 9–1**
- **Light: Full sun to partial shade**
- **Size: 2–3'H×2'W**
- **Features: Blooms in a broad range of colors, early summer**

Siberian iris 'Caesar's Brother'

Unlike bearded iris, Siberian iris's grasslike leaves stay reliably green and lush all summer long. Plants are lovely at the edge of a pond or grouped with lady's mantle or geranium.
Care: Plant Siberian iris in fertile, slightly acidic soil that is continuously moist. Grow in full sun or partial shade. Plant rhizomes in early spring or late summer, spacing them 18 to 24 inches apart. Plants rarely need division. If clumps become crowded or start dying out in the center, divide them in spring or late summer.
Recommended plants and related species: 'Butter and Sugar' is 2 feet tall with white standards (upright petals) and yellow falls (lower petals). 'Caesar's Brother' is the classic, a 3-foot-tall cultivar with dark-violet flowers. 'Fourfold White' is a vigorous white-flowering form. 'Super Ego' is a blue and lavender bicolor. 'My Love' is a rebloomer in the Midwest. Cut old flowering stalks to the ground before seed set to encourage repeat bloom.

Isotoma fluviatilis (Laurentia f., or Pratia pedunculata)
Blue star creeper

- **Hardiness Zones: 5–10**
- **Heat Zones: 10–2**
- **Light: Sun to shade**
- **Size: 1–5"H×24"W**
- **Features: Light blue flowers, late spring and summer**

Blue star creeper has bright evergreen leaves that hug the ground for a mosslike effect. Star-shape flowers grow scattered across the surface of the foliage in late spring and summer. Use it between pavers or stepping-stones, or among rocks. As the plant blankets the soil, it softens these hard materials and blends them into the landscape. With its fine texture and tiny green leaves, blue star creeper also seems at home in woodland gardens, where it will tolerate light foot traffic and bright, dappled light. But plant it with caution. Where conditions are optimum it will form a dense, spreading mat that can ultimately overtake neighboring perennials.
Care: Plant in any well-drained garden soil, ideally one that is normally moist. In areas with hot summers, blue star creeper can be grown in shade. Space plants 6 to 12 inches apart. Water regularly in summer, and fertilize monthly from spring to fall.

Blue star creeper

Kirengeshoma palmata
Yellow waxbells

- **Hardiness Zones: 5–7**
- **Heat Zones: 8–5**
- **Light: Partial to full shade**
- **Size: 2–3'H×3'W**
- **Features: Large, yellow bell-shape flowers bloom for a long season in fall**

Yellow waxbells

Yellow waxbells is a textural delight in shade. It forms a coarse, shrubby mound of maple-leaf-shape foliage. In fall, creamy yellow bells hang from the tips of its stems. Plants grow slowly in clumps. They pair with fine-texture, short, columnar plants, such as Kamchatka bugbane, astilbe, goatsbeard, meadow rue, yellow corydalis, cardinal flower, and globeflower.
Care: Plant in rich, slightly acidic, moist soil. Yellow waxbells does not tolerate heat or drought. It withstands heavy soil and most other conditions if its moisture needs are met. Foliage may scorch in sun or dry soil. Deadhead if desired. In Zones 5 and 6, frost usually ends the bloom period, so seed is rarely set. Plants rarely need division, and staking is unnecessary. Cut plants back in late fall or early spring. Young plants can be mistaken for maple seedlings, so take care not to weed them out. Yellow waxbells is basically pest free.

Knautia macedonica
Knautia

- **Hardiness Zones: 4–9**
- **Heat Zones: 9–1**
- **Light: Full sun**
- **Size: 2'H×2'W**
- **Features: Deep purple-crimson flowers, summer**

Knautia

Knautia is a lovely addition to the border, the cottage garden, or wild garden. Though a somewhat straggly plant, it is charming with its 2-foot-tall, long-lasting, 2-inch flowerheads dancing above low foliage on long, wiry stems. Because the flowering stems may fall over, combine it with more sturdy but open plants, such as meadow sage, that can prop it up. Then its sprays will float beautifully over lower plants. Or try it with other airy bloomers, such as baby's breath and Brazilian verbena.
Care: Grow knautia in full sun and in well-drained soil. It does not tolerate warm nights. Space plants 18 inches apart. Plants start out neat and tidy in spring. In fact, you may think they are spaced too far apart. But, as the summer wears on, the plants spread and can become quite floppy. Knautia sometimes self-sows and is weedy in some situations. Deadheading prevents reseeding. Divide clumps if they become crowded. The flowers attract butterflies and bees.

Kniphofia uvaria
Torch lily

- **Hardiness Zones: 5–9**
- **Heat Zones: 9–1**
- **Light: Full sun**
- **Size: 3–5'H×1–3'W**
- **Features: Showy flower spikes of flamboyant colors, summer to fall**

Torch lily's electric flower spikes stand 3 to 5 feet tall from summer through early fall. It is a showy accent plant, but it's also great for the cut-flower garden.
Care: Torch lily performs best in warm climates. Plant it in full sun in moist, well-drained soil and avoid windy spots. Space plants 18 inches apart. After bloom, cut back spent flower stems by half. In cold-winter regions, mulch roots in early winter to protect them. Plants seldom need division.
Recommended plants and related species: 'Alcazar' bears red flowers with a hint of salmon; it is one of the hardiest cultivars and is a good rebloomer. 'Earliest of All' blooms with orange-red and yellow flowers several weeks earlier than others. 'Ice Queen' has creamy-white flowers on 5-foot-tall plants. 'Shining Sceptre' grows 3 feet tall with golden tangerine flowers. 'Primrose Beauty' is also 3 feet tall and has primrose yellow blooms. All are attractive to hummingbirds.

Torch lily

Lamium maculatum
Spotted dead nettle

- **Hardiness Zones: 3–7**
- **Heat Zones: 8–1**
- **Light: Shade to dense shade**
- **Size: 6–24"H×12–36"W**
- **Features: Colorful foliage and pink, white, or rosy blooms**

Spotted dead nettle 'Chequers'

Spotted dead nettles have a 1- to 3-foot spread, rapidly filling a bed, then setting seed and cropping up in other parts of the yard. Some are weeds; several are fine groundcovers.
Care: Grow spotted dead nettle in a site with cool, moist soil. Space plants 18 to 24 inches apart. (Silver-leaf cultivars grow more slowly; plant them 10 to 15 inches apart.) They do not tolerate winter moisture or very dry soil and hot weather. Plants are less likely to be invasive in dry soil. Shear or mow them in midsummer.
Recommended plants and related species: 'Purple Dragon' is a new cultivar that features silver leaves and purple flowers. 'White Nancy' forms mats of silvery green leaves with small snow-white flowers from late spring to summer. 'Pink Pewter' is similar but with pink flowers. 'Chequers' has mauve-pink flowers and white-striped leaves.

Lavandula angustifolia
English lavender

- **Hardiness Zones: 5–9**
- **Heat Zones: 12–7**
- **Light: Full sun**
- **Size: 1–3'H×1–3'W**
- **Features: Purple flower spikes with seductive fragrance, in early summer**

English lavender

English lavender is a woody perennial for the senses. Both its tiny purple or gray-white flowers and its foliage are fragrant. On a warm day, the scent wafts to people standing nearby. The clump-forming plants grow in a mound of gray foliage at a slow to moderate pace. Attractive companions include taller plants with coarser textures, or plants with blue-green or maroon foliage, such as mullein or coral bells.
Care: Plant in well-drained, sandy soil. English lavender tolerates drought, heat, and wind, but not high humidity, wet soil, or poor drainage. Shear plants after bloom to promote density and repeat bloom. In spring, wait until new growth has begun before cutting plants back; never cut them down to the ground. Propagate by seed or tip cuttings in spring.
Recommended plants and related species: 'Alba' is a small plant with white flowers. 'Munstead' is blue-violet; 'Hidcote Blue' is violet. 'Lavender Lady' is a dwarf and repeats bloom.

Lespedeza thunbergii
Thunberg bush clover

- **Hardiness Zones: 4–9**
- **Heat Zones: Not rated**
- **Light: Full to half sun**
- **Size: 3–6'H×5'W**
- **Features: Plants resemble a miniature wisteria with tiny pink, rose, or white flowers in fall**

Tiny, pretty, pealike flowers coat the stems of thunberg bush clover. For most of the summer, the strong columnar shape forms an upright accent in the garden. But when the flowers appear, the plant becomes a fountain of bloom. Plants grow in clumps at a slow to moderate rate.
Care: Once established in deep and well-drained soil, thunberg bush clover tolerates drought, heat, wind, and a wide soil pH range. Cut plants to the ground or to live wood in early spring; doing so delays blooming. Deadhead to prolong bloom; flowers grow as a multicluster. Plants often benefit from the support of a stake or other tall plant to lean against. Bush clover rarely needs division, a difficult task with this plant. It is basically pest free, but leafhoppers may disfigure foliage in spring and early summer.
Recommended plants and related species: 'Gibraltar' is a floriferous pink-flowered form. In bloom, it arches nearly to the ground.

Thunberg bush clover

Leucanthemum ×superbum
Shasta daisy

- **Hardiness Zones: 4–8**
- **Heat Zones: 9–2**
- **Light: Full to half sun**
- **Size: 10–36"H×24"W**
- **Features: White daisies, early summer**

Shasta daisy

This is the classic white daisy with the yellow center that everyone knows and appreciates.
Care: Plant in any well-drained soil, even one that is moderately alkaline. Deadhead to prolong bloom and to prevent excessive self-sowing. Some varieties repeat bloom if cut back before seed is set. Support taller varieties with grow-through stakes. Fertilize regularly, and divide clumps every two to three years in fall or spring; they have offsets and are easy to move. Discard the oldest, central portion of plant to help control pest buildup—you'll still have many divisions from each clump. Deer usually leave plants alone.
Recommended plants and related species: 'Becky' (2 feet high) and 'Phyllis Smith' (3 feet high) are the best bloomers, both beginning in June and, with deadheading, lasting into August. Most other varieties bloom in June only. All make ideal June wedding flowers. 'May Queen' ox-eye daisy (*L. vulgare* 'Maikönigin') is hardy to Zone 3, blooms in midspring, and reblooms after cutting back.

Liatris spicata
Liatris

- **Hardiness Zones: 3–9**
- **Heat Zones: 9–2**
- **Light: Full sun**
- **Size: 18–60"H×24"W**
- **Features: Bottlebrush-shape flowers of purple or white appear midsummer and are attractive to butterflies**

Liatris

A favorite native of prairies and wet meadows, liatris' bold flowers stand tall. Its unique purple or white flowers are beautiful and long lasting, whether in the garden or a vase. **Care:** Plant in rich soil that is continuously moist (or nearly so). Plants tolerate heat and wind. Prevent drought; it causes reduced bloom and leads to early dormancy. Plants are basically pest-free, though voles may eat the cormlike roots during winter. Liatris self-sows. Tall varieties need staking in average to dry soil. Cut down plants in late fall or early spring. Divide them in fall or spring every four to five years. **Recommended plants and related species:** 'Kobold', 18 to 24 inches, is lilac-mauve. 'August Glory', 3 to 4 feet, is purple-blue. The flowers of rough gayfeather (*L. aspera*) grow in tufts along 3 to 6 feet tall wands. Kansas gayfeather (*L. pycnostachya*), 5 feet tall, takes dry soil. Older clumps often need support. Divide every other year.

Ligularia
Ligularia

- **Hardiness Zones: 5–8**
- **Heat Zones: 8–1**
- **Light: Full to half sun**
- **Size: 30"H×36"W**
- **Features: Showy foliage and flowers in cheerful yellows and oranges, mid- to late summer**

Most ligularias stage their best performance in regions with cool nights. Their large, coarse leaves provide drama. **Care:** Plant in well-drained but constantly moist soil. Mix in plenty of organic matter. Plants need full sun in cool regions and half shade where weather is hot. Space plants 2 to 3 feet apart. Water abundantly and feed regularly. Ligularias will wilt, even when soil seems to have plenty of water. If the soil is moist, they'll recover at sundown. **Recommended plants and related species:** Bigleaf ligularia (*L. dentata*) has large, kidney-shape leaves and daisylike flowers. 'Desdemona' has reddish orange, flowers and deep purple leaves. 'Britt-Marie Crawford' has purple leaves, and 'Othello' has orange flowers and mahogany red leaves. 'Little Lantern' grows to only 2½ feet tall. 'The Rocket' ligularia (*L. stenocephala*) has impressive spikes of bright yellow flowers.

Ligularia

Limonium latifolium
Sea lavender

- **Hardiness Zones: 3–9**
- **Heat Zones: 12–3**
- **Light: Full sun to half sun**
- **Size: 2'H×2'W**
- **Features: Lavender flowers come mid- to late summer and are excellent dried**

Sea lavender

Sea lavender is lovely in the middle of the border. It has a bushy yet see-through habit and airy, flat-topped flower clusters that are attractive in fresh or dried cut-flower arrangements. Its upright stems rise from a clump of big, leathery green basal leaves that turn bright red in fall. **Care:** Plant in well-drained, sandy soil, and in full to half sun. Avoid overfertilizing or overwatering, which lead to lanky growth that requires staking. Space plants 18 to 24 inches apart to ensure good air circulation. Sea lavender is both salt- and heat-tolerant. It is slow to flower after planting. The second year, the plant may put up three or four stalks, but it could be two to three years before you see the plant fully flower. **Recommended plants and related species:** 'Blue Cloud' has light blue blooms; those of 'Violetta' are deep violet-blue. Seafoam (*L. perezii*) is a similar but tender perennial useful in beach plantings in California (Zones 8 to 11).

Linum perenne
Perennial flax

- Hardiness Zones: 5–8
- Heat Zones: 8–2
- Light: Full to half sun
- Size: 18–24"H×12"W
- Features: Blue, blue-violet, or white flowers, late spring to early summer

Perennial flax

This charming, airy, vase-shape plant is a mass of 1-inch flowers. A fast-growing perennial, it's useful as a filler among dense-foliage plants.
Care: Plant perennial flax in well-drained, sandy soil. It is tolerant of heat, drought, and a wide soil pH range, but it does not perform well in wet or poorly drained soil. Deadhead to prolong bloom. Remove each flower stem when there are more seedpods forming below the open flowers than buds developing above them. Plants are pest free but short lived. They self sow. Division is difficult, and perennial flax may not reestablish. However, seedlings are easy to move. Cut plants back in late fall or early spring.
Recommended plants and related species: 'Album' has white flowers. Longer-lived than perennial flax, golden flax (*L. flavum*) has butter yellow flowers on 18-inch-tall stems. 'Compactum' measures 6 to 9 inches tall. 'Heavenly Blue' (*L. narbonense*), 12 to 18 inches tall, has white-eye blue flowers.

Lobelia cardinalis
Cardinal flower

- Hardiness Zones: 3–9
- Heat Zones: 9–2
- Light: Full sun to shade
- Size: 4'H×1'W
- Features: Red flower spikes mid- to late summer, attractive to hummingbirds

Native to wet woods and low meadows, cardinal flower is a short-lived plant that self-sows. Tall spikes of brilliant red flowers top 3- to 4-feet-tall stems anchored by a 12- to 18-inch-wide clump of foliage.
Care: Plant cardinal flower in rich, moist soil. Plants thrive in full sun to shade, but the more sun they receive, the more water they need. Plants grow in bogs but languish in ordinary soil and average water. Deadhead to prolong bloom. Divide every three or four years; spreads by offsets. Cut plants back in late fall or early spring.
Recommended plants and related species: The hybrid 'Ruby Slippers' has beet red blooms. Big blue lobelia (*L. siphilitica*) is 2 to 3 feet tall, with spiky midsummer blue blooms; it needs half sun in Zones 4 to 8, and is more tolerant of dry soil. Hybrid lobelia (*L. ×speciosa*) grows 2 to 3 feet tall and 1 foot wide. Red-violet, fuchsia, pink, white, and blue-violet flowers appear during its long bloom season in Zones 5 to 8.

Cardinal flower

Lupinus Russell Hybrids
Hybrid lupine

- Hardiness Zones: 4–9
- Heat Zones: 6–1
- Light: Full sun to half sun
- Size: 15–36"H×15–24"W
- Features: Wide range of flower colors and bicolors in early summer

Hybrid lupine

Hybrid lupine produces fabulous, showy flowers. They are best massed in beds or when combined with geraniums or shasta daisy.
Care: Hybrid lupines thrive in rich, moist, well-drained soil. They perform best where summers are cool. Lupine will not grow well in hot, humid summers or where wet, cold winters exist. Provide rich, moist soil and good drainage. Space plants 18 to 24 inches apart. Water during dry periods. Mulch in summer to keep roots cool. Use a lightweight mulch in winter where snow cover is not reliable. Plants need no staking. Powdery mildew, rust, aphids, and four-line plant bugs can be problems.
Recommended plants and related species: Gallery Hybrids, a dwarf series, are 15 to 18 inches tall, with blue, pink, red, and white blooms. Minarette Hybrids, also dwarf at 18 to 20 inches, are a mix of colors. 'My Castle' has brick red flowers on 2- to 3-foot-tall plants. 'The Chatelaine' (Band of Nobles Series) has pink and white bicolor flowers.

Macleaya cordata
Plume poppy

- **Hardiness Zones: 3–8**
- **Heat Zones: 12–7**
- **Light: Full sun or half sun**
- **Size: 6–10'H×6'W**
- **Features: Creamy plumes of flowers in early summer**

Plume poppy

This huge plant, with its 10- to 12-inch airy plumes and hairy, heart-shape leaves, is impressive for large gardens. Use it as a living screen, or at the back of an expansive border. Plants are potentially weedy, particularly if soil is rich and moist. Combine it with other equally gigantic plants, such as joe-pye weed.
Care: Plant plume poppy in any well-drained soil. Plume poppies require little care where there is room to spread. Plant them in full sun or part shade. (Plants decline in full shade.) Allow 6 feet between plants. Install a barrier to keep roots from spreading beyond the allotted area, if necessary. Staking isn't needed. Divide plants every two years or as needed to reduce crowding among clumps. Take care working with plants as their yellow sap stains clothes.
Recommended plants and related species: 'Flamingo' is a pink-flower variety on gray-green stems. 'Coral Plume' *(M. microcarpa)* is similar to plume poppy and reaches up to 8 feet tall with showy coral pink blossoms.

Malva alcea
Hollyhock mallow

- **Hardiness Zones: 4–10**
- **Heat Zones: 8–1**
- **Light: Full sun to half sun**
- **Size: 3–4'H×3'W**
- **Features: Purplish pink flowers, summer to frost**

Hollyhock mallow is an easy, handsome plant that brightens the garden for most of the summer. It is free-flowering, tall, and bushy with heart-shape, scalloped leaves and funnel-shape, purplish pink flowers.
Care: Plant hollyhock mallow in any well-drained soil in full sun. In regions with hot summers, plant in half sun. Space plants 18 inches apart or sow seeds in spring. Cut back plant tops 12 inches after the first flush of bloom to promote continued blossoming and prevent self-sowing, which can get out of hand. Avoid overhead irrigation to prevent powdery mildew.
Recommended plants and related species: 'Fastigiata' has attractive deep pink flowers well into autumn; it has a more compact, neat, upright form. 'Zebrina' *(M. sylvestris)* has strong, erect stems and white to pink flowers with raspberry red markings. A short-lived perennial, often treated as an annual, it has flowers that resemble pinwheels all summer. The plant is hardy to Zone 5.

Hollyhock mallow

Matteuccia struthiopteris
Ostrich fern

- **Hardiness Zones: 2–7**
- **Heat Zones: 8–1**
- **Light: Shade to sun**
- **Size: 3'H×3'W**
- **Features: Large, light green fronds**

Ostrich fern

If you want the classic fern look, ostrich fern is your choice. It naturalizes beautifully in dappled shade. Unsurpassed for its dramatic fronds that resemble ostrich feathers, this big, bold, vase-shape perennial spreads rapidly and is perfect growing in mass plantings. It is the source of edible fiddleheads in spring, and its roots spread rapidly. In many gardens, ostrich fern may be too aggressive to combine with other perennials, unless you have the time to dig out the extra plants that appear as it naturalizes.
Care: Plants grow well in average to moist soil. Although best in shade, ostrich fern will tolerate sun as long as the soil never dries out. Space plants 3 feet apart. Ostrich fern does not perform well in the hot summers of the South. Its fronds will scorch if the soil becomes too dry, even in shade.

Miscanthus sinensis
Miscanthus

- Hardiness Zones: 4–9
- Heat Zones: 9–1
- Light: Full sun
- Size: 3–7'H×3'W
- Features: Ornamental grass with large pink or silver flower plumes in fall

This outstanding grass—valued for its foliage and flowers—forms dense clumps that may be tall and narrow or fountain-shape. Miscanthus flowers begin as drooping purplish fans. These open to long, silky spikelets that mature in late summer to dazzling silvery plumes and last well into winter.

Care: Miscanthus flops in shade. It thrives in moderate to wet conditions and tolerates drought. Allow 4 to 5 feet between plants. Divide plants as they outgrow their boundaries. Cut them back in early spring. Miscanthus mealybug can be a problem.

Recommended plants and related species: In warmer regions (Zones 6 to 9) choose cultivars that flower late to prevent self-sowing. Plant only named cultivars; the species is not as ornamental and readily self-sows. 'Gracillimus' grows 4 to 6 feet tall, with

Miscanthus 'Zebrinus'

narrow, curling leaves. A late bloomer, it may not flower in Zones 5 and colder. Flame grass ('Purpurascens') has orange-red fall color and silvery plumes. 'Morning Light' has white-striped leaves and 4- to 6-feet-tall flower stems. Zebra grass ('Zebrinus') is upright (5 to 7 feet tall) with horizontal yellow bands on the leaves. Porcupine grass ('Strictus') is shorter (4 to 6 feet tall) but more erect. 'Adagio' is a dwarf, growing up to 3 feet tall and wide.

Miscanthus 'Gracillimus'

Molinia caerulea 'Variegata'
Variegated purple moor grass

- Hardiness Zones: 3–9
- Heat Zones: 9–1
- Light: Full sun to half sun
- Size: 18"H×18"W
- Features: Ornamental grass has yellow and green foliage; compact form

Variegated purple moor grass

Native to moist, cool, acidic soils, sometimes called moorlands, this graceful deciduous grass forms dense tufts. This is an elegant ornamental grass because of its refined habit and fall beauty. Use it as a groundcover, an edger, or a showy specimen.

Care: Grow variegated purple moor grass in full sun in acid to neutral, moderately moist soil. Space plants 2 feet apart. In Southern regions, grow it in half sun. Divide plants when they outgrow their boundaries. Large varieties require cutting back; smaller ones lose their leaves in fall.

Recommended plants and related species: Tall purple moor grass (*M. c. arundinacea*) has fine-texture foliage only 2 to 3 feet tall, but its flowers, appearing high above, arch out 7 to 8 feet high. 'Skyracer' is 7 to 8 feet tall, with more erect stems and attractive yellow-orange fall color.

Monarda didyma
Bee balm

- ■ **Hardiness Zones:** 4–9
- ■ **Heat Zones:** 9–2
- ■ **Light:** Half to full sun
- ■ **Size:** 3–6'H×2–4'W
- ■ **Features:** Lilac, pink, red, or white flowers, early summer

Bee balm

Bee balm is one of the best plants for attracting hummingbirds and butterflies, but it can be invasive. The fast-growing plants are columnar in bloom, forming a low mat before bloom. They combine well with miscanthus, goatsbeard, astilbe, and hardy hibiscus.

Care: Plant bee balm in well-drained soil that has a neutral to slightly acidic pH. Plants don't tolerate drought or high humidity. Deadhead to prolong bloom. Stake with grow-through supports or cut plants back one or two times before they bloom. Powdery mildew can be serious; grow only resistant varieties. Four-lined plant bug disfigures foliage. Divide or remove excess plants every two to three years; they spread by offsets and are easy to move. Cut back in late winter or early spring.

Recommended plants and related species: Mildew-resistant cultivars, shades of red: 'Jacob Cline', 'Raspberry Wine'; shades of purple: 'Violet Queen', 'Petite Delight', 'Vintage Wine'; shades of pink: 'Marshall's Delight'.

Muhlenbergia capillaris
Gulf muhly

- ■ **Hardiness Zones:** 6–10
- ■ **Heat Zones:** 12–1
- ■ **Light:** Full sun to half sun
- ■ **Size:** 1–3'H×1–2'W
- ■ **Features:** Vibrant pink to pink-purple flower plumes, late summer

This fine-textured grass is suited to beds or naturalistic settings. It grows 1 to 3 feet tall and even larger in rich soil. In late summer, the grass sends out light purple plumes that fade to gold in the fall. Grow it as an accent or a groundcover; this well-behaved beauty is at home anywhere you would plant an ornamental grass. Its structure adds interest to the winter garden.

Care: This tough native plant tolerates wet or sandy soil, sunny or partially shaded sites. It is resistant to salt sprays and is basically pest free. The plant rarely needs division. Gulf muhly draws butterflies.

Recommended plants and related species: Bamboo muhly *(M. dumosa)* provides the graceful airiness of clumping bamboo. It reaches 4 feet high or more in a single season. Thin blue leaves of Texas native *(M. lindheimeri)* grow 15 inches long with contrasting purplish flowers. Both are hardy to Zone 7.

Gulf muhly

Myosotis palustris
(M. scorpioides)
True forget-me-not

- ■ **Hardiness Zones:** 3–8
- ■ **Heat Zones:** Not rated
- ■ **Light:** Half sun to shade
- ■ **Size:** 6–8"H×8"W
- ■ **Features:** Tiny, baby blue flowers, mid- to late spring

True forget-me-not

Carpets of tiny, baby blue flowers with yellow centers characterize this ground-hugging perennial. It grows very fast, spreading 18 inches or more a year. Use it as an edging for the front of gardens. True forget-me-not also works as a pretty spacer among moisture-loving plants requiring half-sun and good air circulation, such as bee balm, garden phlox, or globeflower. Some cultivars can also grow in the water of a pond or stream.

Care: Plant in soil that is rich in organic matter. Plants do not tolerate heat or drought; full sun is OK only if soil is wet. Plants self-sow prolifically, but not offensively. Cut plants back as desired each spring to keep them within bounds. Remove oldest portions every three to four years, and allow remaining plants to recolonize the renewed soil. Though pest-free, plants can succumb to crown rot, which kills patches in mid- to late summer in hot areas or where the soil is dry.

Nepeta × faassenii
Catmint

- ▥ **Hardiness Zones: 4–8**
- ▥ **Heat Zones: 12–2**
- ▥ **Light: Full to half sun**
- ▥ **Size: 1–2'H×2'W**
- ▥ **Features: Blue-violet flowers, midspring to early fall**

Catmint

An important source of blue for the front of a garden, catmint produces billowing masses of small flowers for several weeks. The fast-growing plants are mounded clump-formers with scented gray-green foliage.
Care: Catmint grows well in any well-drained soil of average moisture. Plants tolerate heat, wind, drought, and foot traffic. Deadhead by shearing after spring bloom. Where seasons are longer, shearing after follow-up blooms can allow another flower cycle. Divide plants every five to six years to renew vigor. Cut plants back in early spring.
Recommended plants and related species: 'Blue Wonder' has deep blue-violet flowers and is only 12 to 15 inches tall and wide. 'Walker's Low' is even more compact. A sterile hybrid, N. ×faassenii is sometimes confused with look-alike relatives such as N. racemosa, which is a prolific self-sower. N. subsessilis, Zones 5 to 9, grows upright and plants aren't floppy.

Oenothera fruticosa
Common sundrops

- ▥ **Hardiness Zones: 4–9**
- ▥ **Heat Zones: 12–1**
- ▥ **Light: Full to half sun**
- ▥ **Size: 18–24"H×18–24"W**
- ▥ **Features: Yellow flowers, early to midsummer**

A fast-growing, upright spreader, common sundrops reaches its maximum size within one to two years. Yellow flowers sit on sturdy stems. Its basal rosettes are evergreen and turn maroon in cold weather.
Care: Plant common sundrops in any well-drained soil. Deadhead to prolong bloom and to prevent self-sowing. Then, when blooming stops, shear plants back by one-third. Divide plants in spring or early fall every four to five years. Remove and discard the oldest, central portion of the clump.
Recommended plants and related species: The yellow flowers, red buds, and reddish stems of 'Fireworks' are eye-catching. Ozark sundrops (O. macrocarpa) is a sprawling plant with long-lasting lemon yellow flowers. Though the plant grows less than 12 inches tall, its stems spread 18 inches in Zones 4 to 8. Showy evening primrose (O. speciosa), 18 inches tall, has enchanting daytime blooms that open white and fade to pink in Zones 5 to 8. It is a mildly invasive groundcover.

Common sundrops

Ophiopogon japonicus
Mondo grass

- ▥ **Hardiness Zones: 6–10**
- ▥ **Heat Zones: 12–1**
- ▥ **Light: Sun to partial shade**
- ▥ **Size: 6–12"H×12"W**
- ▥ **Features: Grassy clumps with small lilac flowers, late summer**

Black mondo grass 'Niger'

Not a true grass, but resembling ornamental grasses in appearance and behavior, this unusual foliage plant is a standout, especially when contrasted with brighter colors. It spreads slowly and grows about a foot high. It has slender, shiny, dark evergreen leaves and small tubular flowers on spiky stalks. Small, blue, pea-size fruit follow the blooms. It is a good edging for beds and paths.
Care: Mondo grass prefers fertile, moist, humus-rich, well-drained soil. It can be grown in sun or light shade, but requires moist soil in sun. Mow or cut it back in spring before new growth begins. In full sun, mondo grass needs more frequent watering. Divide plants in spring when they become crowded. Mondo grass is usually pest free. Space plants 12 inches apart.
Recommended plants and related species: Black mondo grass (O. planiscapus 'Niger') forms clumps of purple-black foliage up to 9 inches tall. It has evergreen leaves and white or lilac flowers.

Origanum laevigatum
Ornamental oregano

- **Hardiness Zones: 5–9**
- **Heat Zones: 10–2**
- **Light: Full sun**
- **Size: 12–24"H×18"W**
- **Features: Long-lasting purple to pink flowers, late summer**

Ornamental oregano 'Herrenhausen'

A mainstay of herb gardens, oregano has some lovely vibrant-blooming cousins. Their foliage is fragrant, but unlike that of the herb. Use ornamental oregano at the front of beds and borders or let plants weave through other perennials.

Care: Grow ornamental oregano in full sun in average, well-drained soil, spacing plants at least a foot apart. Avoid wet sites; ornamental oregano cannot tolerate wet feet. Keep plants tidy and compact by cutting them back by about half in early summer. Some cultivars need winter mulch to survive in areas colder than Zone 6.

Recommended plants and related species: 'Herrenhausen' is one of the most ornamental, with abundant sprays of maroon flowers and reddish purple-tinged foliage. Hybrids may bloom earlier: 'Hopleys', 18 inches tall and wide, lavender to deep blue flowers; 'Rosenkuppel', erect form, bright pink to mauve flowers; and 'Nymphenburg', 20 inches tall, pink flowers.

Osmunda cinnamomea
Cinnamon fern

- **Hardiness Zones: 3–7**
- **Heat Zones: 8–1**
- **Light: Shade to full sun**
- **Size: 36"H×18"W**
- **Features: Stately, tall fern fronds**

Robust and elegant in form, cinnamon fern is a good choice for sunny, low-lying spots—ideal at the water's edge or where water stands—and for cool areas. Its fertile fronds emerge in spring, changing to cinnamon-brown, hence the name.

Care: Plant cinnamon fern in moist soil that has an acidic pH. Plant 2 feet apart in light shade or full sun. Plants are pest-free.

Recommended plants and related species: One of the largest garden ferns, royal fern *(O. regalis)* is typically 4 to 6 feet tall but can grow taller in wet areas. It's fairly sun tolerant if it receives an adequate supply of moisture.

Cinnamon fern

Osteospermum hybrids
Osteospermum

- **Hardiness Zones: 9–11**
- **Heat Zones: 12–1**
- **Light: Full sun**
- **Size: 8–15"H×12–15"W**
- **Features: Continuously blooming, low-growing perennial**

Osteospermum

Native to southern Africa, osteospermum is woody at its base and grows in a mounding and trailing fashion. White, purple, pink, and sometimes pale yellow flowers cover the plants mostly in spring and fall, but intermittently throughout summer. The sunlight-sensitive flowers close partially in the evening or during cloudy weather. Plants are frost tender but grow fast, so are easy to enjoy as summer annuals.

Care: Plant in any well-drained soil. Osteospermum can tolerate extended periods of little or no water, but looks best with regular irrigation. Pinch growing tips to promote bushy, flowerful growth.

Recommended plants and related species: The Symphony Series comes in orange, yellow, pale yellow, and peach. 'Soprano Purple' is dark purple. *O. jucundum* 'Purple Mountain' also produces purple flowers, but is hardy to Zone 5, and it grows taller.

Paeonia lactiflora
Chinese peony

- Hardiness Zones: 3–7
- Heat Zones: 9–1
- Light: Full to half sun
- Size: 3'H×3'W
- Features: White, pink, red, lilac, and bicolor flowers, often fragrant, late spring to early summer; many have attractive bronze-yellow leaves in fall

A stalwart of the perennial garden, Chinese peony provides beauty that lasts a lifetime. The large flowers may be single, double, or one of many intermediate forms. Substantial plants can easily stand alone but look grand surrounded by low-growing, fine-textured perennials. Chinese peonies have long-lasting foliage that serves as background, filler, and support for later-blooming perennials, such as meadow rue, balloon flower, and Japanese anemone.

A hedge of Chinese peonies

'Blaze' Chinese peony

Care: Chinese peonies can live for decades, so planting them right, in deep, well-drained soil, pays dividends. Plants tolerate a wide pH range but will not grow in lean, dry soil, or in windy situations. Their large flowers are almost too heavy for their stems to hold up. Deadhead to reduce the weight; this won't extend bloom or encourage new flowers. Stake with grow-through supports or hoops in early spring. Fertilize in spring when shoots are emerging. Divide plants in fall every 8 to 10 years to renew the planting and the soil. Plant the divisions so that the large pinkish buds are only 1 to 2 inches below the soil's surface, spacing them 3 feet apart. Peonies will not flower until plants have been chilled to below 40°F for several months. For this reason, they do not bloom well in regions with warm winters. Botrytis infection is common; dark spots on leaves, purple-brown streaks on stems, and small, dried, unopened flower buds are symptoms. Good sanitation prevents spread of the disease and eventual decline of the plant. Remove all discolored foliage as you see it and clean up all foliage in late fall to avoid infecting new shoots as they emerge in spring. Check roots and discard any that are distorted or soft. Spent petals can host botrytis infection.

Recommended plants and related species: Hundreds of beautiful varieties are available. Pick by color, fragrance, or other attribute. For instance, single flowers are lighter, so usually they can remain upright without staking. Double-flower kinds are heavier, more formal, and more traditional.

'Sarah Bernhardt' Chinese peony

Panicum virgatum
Switch grass

- Hardiness Zones: 3–9
- Heat Zones: 9–1
- Light: Full sun
- Size: 3–6'H×2–6'W
- Features: Ornamental grass with airy dark purple to pink flowers, fall

Switch grass 'Heavy Metal'

This native prairie grass makes an excellent fall and winter display. Its blue-green leaves form an upright column that turns bright yellow or red in fall. A fine-texture grass, it is beautiful as a specimen or a living screen.
Care: Switch grass prefers moist soil but will grow in sand or clay. Plants tolerate half sun, dry sites, and seaside conditions. In shaded sites, they may need staking. Space plants 3 feet apart. Cut them back in late winter. Switch grass is usually pest free.
Recommended plants and related species: Upright 'Northwind' is one of the best cultivars. 'Cloud Nine' forms a cloud of seedheads above the foliage; 6 feet tall and wide. 'Heavy Metal' has upright, metallic blue leaves that turn amber yellow in fall. 'Haense Herms' ('Rotstrahlbusch') or red switch grass is the reddest variety, 3 feet tall and 4 feet wide. 'Strictum' has 5- to 6-foot-tall blue leaves. 'Shenandoah' has reddish purple foliage.

Papaver orientale
Oriental poppy

- Hardiness Zones: 3–8
- Heat Zones: 8–3
- Light: Full sun
- Size: 3'H×2'W
- Features: Red, orange, pink, or white flowers, mid- to late spring

Fabulous flowers open in mid- to late spring but finish blooming all too soon. Plants grow at a moderate to fast rate. Because they go dormant after blooming, grow oriental poppies with late-emerging perennials to cover the poppies' fading foliage.
Care: Plant in locations that drain well but are rich in organic matter. Avoid sites with high wind or wet soil. Deadhead to keep the planting neat, or allow seedpods to develop to use in dried decorations. Foliage begins growth in mid- to late summer and persists through winter. Refrain from cutting it back in late fall. Leaves resume growth in early spring and are already dying back by early summer to enter a short summer dormancy. Oriental poppy rarely needs division, and the forked taproot is hard to move. To propagate, dig the fleshy taproots after flowering. Plants will grow from root cuttings as well as from bits of roots left behind in digging.

Oriental poppy

Patrinia scabiosifolia
Yellow patrinia

- Hardiness Zones: 4–9
- Heat Zones: 12–1
- Light: Full to half sun
- Size: 3–6'H×2'W
- Features: Yellow-green flower clusters, mid- to late summer

Yellow patrinia

You can count on this plant to bloom with yellow, cup-shape flowers from summer to fall. It goes well with just about everything in a garden. The airy, flat-top, flower clusters on sturdy stems resemble a grouping of queen anne's lace. Yellow patrinia is a clump-forming plant that spreads by stolons at a moderate rate. During summer heat, its blooms recall cool spring green.
Care: Plants tolerate wind, heat, drought, and humidity, but not winter-wet soil. They are basically pest-free. Avoid deadheading in the first year. Plants will self-sow. Divide them every four to five years to maintain vigor; plants spread by offsets. Cut plants back in late fall or early spring.
Recommended plants and related species: 'Nagoya' grows 3 feet tall and 2 feet wide. The 12- to 18-inch mound of basal leaves differs in appearance from the feathery stem leaves. Flowering stems arise from established roots, so outer edges of a clump and new transplants may not flower.

Pennisetum alopecuroides
Perennial fountain grass

- **Hardiness Zones: 5–9**
- **Heat Zones: 9–1**
- **Light: Full sun to light shade in the South; full sun elsewhere**
- **Size: 2–4'H×2'W**
- **Features: Glossy green blades and bottlebrush blooms, late summer**

Perennial fountain grass 'Hameln'

One of the most useful grasses for flower gardens, perennial fountain grass is a warm-season grass that looks good all year. Its narrow, fine-texture, glossy green leaves form a dense mass that remains green into fall, then changes to rose, apricot, or gold before bleaching almond for winter. In late summer, its foxtaillike plumes appear.

Care: Perennial fountain grass is well adapted and easy to grow in any well-drained soil. Space plants 3 feet apart. Cut plants to the ground in the fall.

Recommended plants and related species: 'Hameln' is smaller and finer than the common species. It grows 2 feet tall and wide. 'Little Bunny' is shorter and suits rock gardens. 'Moudry' is 30 inches tall with deep green leaves and black flowers in fall. *P. orientale* 'Karley Rose' grows 3 to 3½ feet tall with dark green leaves and pink flowers. It's hardy in Zones 5 to 8.

Penstemon barbatus
Common beard tongue

- **Hardiness Zones: 4–9**
- **Heat Zones: 9–1**
- **Light: Full to half sun**
- **Size: 4–30"H×12–18"W**
- **Features: White, pink, red, purple, or blue flowers, early summer**

Common beard tongues include spectacular western wildflowers as well as species suitable for gardens, in hot, humid regions. The species has tubular scarlet flowers, while hybrids have larger blooms. Until plants bloom, they form a neat mat. Combine common beard tongue with artemisia, pearly everlasting, Chinese peony, Japanese water iris, dropwort, bloody cranesbill, feather reed grass, fountain grass, or catmint. Pair dark-stem cultivars with pink-flower daylilies or hardy hibiscus.

Care: Plant common beard tongue in any well-drained soil. Plants tolerate heat and wind. Avoid sites with wet soil in winter. Space plants 1 to 2 feet apart, depending on the cultivar's mature size. Deadhead to prolong bloom. Divide plants every four to five years to maintain vigor; they have offsets and are easy to move. Plants self-sow. Seedlings are variable but worth watching for.

Common beard tongue 'Prairie Dusk'

Large-flower beard tongue

Cut plants back in late fall or early spring. Well-grown plants can be sturdy and attractive through winter. Seedheads dry well but have an unpleasant smell. The plants are basically pest free; leaf spot and nematodes may trouble older clumps.

Recommended plants and related species: The Prairie Series of hybrids are evergreen in warm regions. 'Prairie Dusk' has clear purple blooms; 'Prairie Fire' is red; 'Elfin Pink' has pink blooms. 'Husker Red' *(P. digitalis)* has cool white flowers along tall maroon stems in late spring to early summer. Foliage may fade to bronze or green in summer heat; it grows to 2 to 3 feet in Zones 2 to 7. Tender hybrids: 'Garnet', wine-red blooms, 30 inches; 'Sour Grapes', bunched blue-violet flowers, 18 to 24 inches (Zones 7 to 10). Large-flowered beard tongue *(P. grandiflorus)* produces large flowers on 4-foot-tall stalks.

Perovskia atriplicifolia
Russian sage

- **Hardiness Zones:** 3–9
- **Heat Zones:** 9–2
- **Light:** Full sun
- **Size:** 3–5'H×3–4'W
- **Features:** Tiny lavender-blue flowers, mid- to late summer

Russian sage 'Blue Spire'

Tiny flowers fleck fragrant gray stems in mid- to late summer. A shrubby perennial with lacy gray-green leaves, Russian sage spreads by natural layering. Its growth rate is moderate (but plants can become invasive in mild climates). Russian sage creates a silvery effect, and combines well with grasses and other large-scale perennials.
Care: Plant Russian sage in well-drained, sandy or gravelly soil. Plants tolerate heat, drought, alkaline soil, and wind. Fertilize at half the average rate. Cut previous year's branches to their base in early spring after buds break to promote upright new growth and better flowering. Stake plants in moist, rich soil. Plants rarely require division but may need protective winter mulch around branch bases in Zones 3 to 4 if there's no snow cover.
Recommended plants and related species: 'Blue Spire' (also called 'Longin') has deeper violet flowers and grows more upright than the species. 'Little Spire' is shorter and more upright.

Persicaria affinis
(Polygonum affine)
Himalayan fleeceflower

- **Hardiness Zones:** 3–7
- **Heat Zones:** 8–1
- **Light:** Full sun to partial shade
- **Size:** 8–14"H×24"W
- **Features:** Rosy red flower spikes in summer and early fall

Himalayan fleeceflower is one of the good-looking, well-behaved members of a group of plants called knotweed, which includes a few obnoxious weeds. Bindweed is one example. Unfortunately, this plant is often tarred by the same brush. While the family resemblence is there, Himalayan fleeceflower is never invasive. Its narrow, deep-green leaves form a mat less than a foot high. In summer, numerous spikes rise above the leaves, each one packed densely with tiny rosy red flowers. Use it toward the front of a perennial border or as a small-area groundcover.
Care: Himalayan fleeceflower is easy to grow in any soil that is moist and fertile. Shaded locations are okay but full sun will permit growth of a more dense leafy cover and better flowering.
Recommended plants and related species: 'Darjeeling Red' has a lower, denser mat of leaves and 1-inch spikes of deep-pink flowers that age to red. Its leaves turn red in fall. 'Superba' has pink flowers.

Himalayan fleeceflower

Phlox paniculata
Garden phlox

- **Hardiness Zones:** 4–8
- **Heat Zones:** 9–4
- **Light:** Half to full sun
- **Size:** 36–40"H×18–24"W
- **Features:** White, pink, magenta, or lilac flowers, mid- to late summer

Garden phlox 'Natascha'

Today's garden phlox is nothing like the muddy magenta plant found in the wild. Hybridizers have developed plants with spectacular blooms and improved disease resistance.
Care: Plant garden phlox in any well-drained soil. Plants tolerate wind and a wide pH range, but not drought with extreme heat and high humidity. Apply 50 percent more fertilizer than average. Stake tall varieties with grow-through supports. If stems flop, thin clumps and increase water and fertilizer the next spring. Divide plants every three to four years; they have offsets. Plants self-sow readily; seedlings are usually inferior. Cut plants to the ground in late fall and remove trimmings.
Recommended plants and related species: Mildew-resistant cultivars include 'David', white blooms; 'Eva Cullum', bright pink with red eye; 'Franz Schubert', lilac-blue with crimson eye; 'Natascha', pink and white; 'Robert Poore', purple; and 'Shortwood', pink.

Phlox subulata
Moss phlox

- **Hardiness Zones: 2–8**
- **Heat Zones: 9–4**
- **Light: Full sun**
- **Size: 6–8"H×24"W**
- **Features: Masses of pink, red, white or lavender flowers, early to midspring**

Moss phlox

Moss phlox is a magnificent low-growing groundcover that blooms lavishly in sunny gardens from early to midspring. When blooming, the creeping plants are covered with a mass of color. The foliage is prickly and resembles moss. Use moss phlox as a pretty evergreen edging or at the base of shrubs.
Care: Plant moss phlox in any well-drained soil, ideally one with a neutral to slightly alkaline pH. Set clumps a foot apart, and shear plants after they bloom. Thin out clumps whenever they become crowded. Mulch lightly to protect shallow roots, but avoid smothering the evergreen leaves. Divide plants as needed to control their spread.
Recommended plants and related species: 'Candy Stripe' has white flowers striped with pink. 'Emerald Gem' is light pink with a mounding habit. 'Scarlet Flame' is deep red. 'Apple Blossom' has pale pink blooms. 'Red Wings' is a heavy blooming rosy red. 'Snowflake' is the showiest white.

Phormium tenax
New Zealand flax

- **Hardiness Zones: 8–11**
- **Heat Zones: 12–1**
- **Light: Full sun**
- **Size: 5–7'H×4'W**
- **Features: Swordlike, ornamental leaves in rich colors**

Native to the swamps of New Zealand, this plant grows in clumps and has foliage that may be yellow-green, dark green, red, rust-colored, or variegated with many fine stripes. Grown for dramatic effect and colorful foliage, New Zealand flax has limited adaptability but is great as an annual where winters are cold. Plant it at the edge of a water garden, as a focal point in the border, or in a container.
Care: New Zealand flax grows best in deep, fertile, and well-drained soil. Water regularly to keep soil moist. Divide plants in spring.
Recommended plants and related species: 'Aurora' bears leaves striped with red, pink, and yellow. 'Burgundy' is a deep wine red. 'Purpureum' has a purple-red sheen to its leaves. 'Williamsii Variegata' has wide yellow-vein green leaves. Mountain flax (*P. cookianum*) is a smaller, 3-foot plant with pendulous flowers. 'Maori Chief' has bronze leaves streaked with red and pink.

New Zealand flax 'Purpureum'

Platycodon grandiflorus
Balloon flower

- **Hardiness Zones: 3–8**
- **Heat Zones: 9–3**
- **Light: Half to full sun**
- **Size: 1–2'H×2'W**
- **Features: Blue stars of deep blue-violet, white, or pink, early to midsummer**

Balloon flower 'Sentimental Blue'

Balloon flower is named for its inflated blue buds that look like expanding balloons and open into cupped, five-pointed stars. These elegant, fun, and easy plants combine beautifully with almost any perennial.
Care: Plant in any well-drained soil. Balloon flower is slow to emerge in spring, so be patient. Surround it with early bulbs and take care not to hoe it down. You may need to stake the tallest forms as well as plants in shade and in hot regions. Use individual braces for each stem. Deadhead to prolong bloom. Plants are difficult to transplant but rarely need dividing. Propagate by cutting pencil-thick side roots from the main taproot. Balloon flower self-sows but seedlings are variable. Cut plants back in late fall or early spring.
Recommended plants and related species: 'Mariesii', with blue-violet blooms, and 'Shell Pink' have a compact size, 18 to 24 inches tall. 'Sentimental Blue' grows less than 12 inches tall.

Polemonium caeruleum
Jacob's ladder

- **Hardiness Zones: 3–8**
- **Heat Zones: 7–1**
- **Light: Half to full sun**
- **Size: 2'H×1'W**
- **Features: Blue-violet or white flowers, mid- to late spring**

Jacob's ladder

Blue-violet or white flowers cluster at the stem tips of this clump-forming plant, which grows at a moderate to fast rate. The fine-textured foliage and upright-arching shape complement hosta, celandine poppy, and lady's mantle.
Care: Plant jacob's ladder in any soil that is rich in organic matter. Plants tolerate shade and alkalinity. They do not perform well in heat, humidity, or drought. Provide continuous moisture and good drainage for plants that receive more sun. As flowering falls off, cut back hard to encourage new foliage. Divide plants every three to four years in fall or spring. They spread by offsets and are easy to move.
Recommended plants and related species: 'Snow and Sapphires', has white variegated leaves and sky blue fragrant flowers. Leafy jacob's ladder *(P. foliosissimum)* is taller (30 inches) and blooms later. 'Stairway to Heaven' creeping polemonium *(P. reptans)* has variegated leaves and blue flowers.

Polygonatum
Solomon's seal

- **Hardiness Zones: 4–9**
- **Heat Zones: 9–1**
- **Light: Half sun to shade**
- **Size: 1–6'H×1–2'W**
- **Features: Narrow, creamy bells, mid- to late spring, and buttery yellow leaves in fall**

Solomon's seal is highly regarded for its arching stems from which white flowers dangle in spring. The upright-arching form contrasts with mounded hosta, fringe-cup, lungwort, bloody cranesbill, purple-leaf coral bells, and bleeding heart.
Care: Plant solomon's seal in any soil that is rich in organic matter. It does not do well in hot summers and is likely to go dormant early if you try to grow it in warm regions. Divide every five to six years in fall or spring; plants have offsets and are easy to move.
Recommended plants and related species: Small solomon's seal *(P. biflorum)* grows 18 to 36 inches tall. Great solomon's seal *(P. commutatum)* may reach 6 feet. Its foliage turns apricot in fall, so the plant becomes a stately, glowing shrub in the shade garden in Zones 3–8. Foliage of variegated solomon's seal *(P. odoratum* 'Variegatum') is delicately outlined in ivory, and grows 18 to 30 inches tall and wide in Zones 4 to 9.

Solomon's seal

Polystichum
Sword, tassel, and Christmas ferns

- **Hardiness Zones: 4-10, depending on species**
- **Heat Zones: 9–1**
- **Light: Half sun to shade**
- **Size: 1–5'H×1–3'W**
- **Features: Sturdy evergreen fronds**

Sword fern

The lustrous green fronds of these tough, pest-free plants captivate gardeners. Pair with woodland perennials such as yellow corydalis.
Care: Plant these ferns in moist and well-drained soil. Plant container-grown specimens in spring. Space western sword ferns 3 feet apart; tassel ferns 1 foot apart; and Christmas ferns 2 feet apart. Water regularly in dry weather. Divide clumps when crowded. Remove brown foliage as new growth emerges.
Recommended plants and related species: Western sword fern *(P. munitum)* is 1 to 5 feet tall and hardy only to Zone 7; divide in fall. Tassel fern *(P. polyblepharum)* has dark, glossy fronds and grows 1½ to 2 feet tall and 10 inches wide; use in Zones 6 to 8. Christmas fern *(P. acrostichoides)*, 1½ to 2 feet tall, grows best in Zones 4 to 8; divide in spring. The cut fronds are popular for Christmas decorations.

Primula
Primrose

- **Hardiness Zones: 5–8**
- **Heat Zones: 8–1**
- **Light: Part shade; full sun if kept moist**
- **Size: 4–18"H×6–18"W**
- **Features: Clusters of white, red, pink, and yellow flowers**

Japanese primrose

By growing different species, you can have primroses in flower from late winter through midsummer. Although considered the queen of bog garden plants, it languishes in the hot summers of Heat Zone 8 or warmer. Space plants half the distance of their mature width. In early to midsummer, stems bearing whorls of flowers 1 inch across in shades ranging from pure white to deep red grow out of light green rosettes of finely scalloped or serrated, oblong-shape foliage.
Care: Plant primroses in partial shade in rich, moist, neutral to acidic loam. They will tolerate sun if kept uniformly moist. The ideal location receives bright light in early spring and shade in summer, such as under deciduous trees. Divide primroses in early spring. Mulch in spring and deadhead blooms in late spring. Spider mites may be a problem in hot weather. Primroses self-seed freely and over time will make a large colony.

Recommended plants and related species: English primrose (*P. vulgaris*) is considered one of the easiest to grow species, and particularly so for gardeners that live in Zones 8 to 9. It tolerates a bit more heat and drier conditions that most other primroses. Its yellow flowers, often with a darker yellow marking near the eye, are 1-inch-wide and are borne singly atop 9-inch stems. Other flower colors, including pink and purple, are found in some subspecies and cultivars. This primrose is most stunning when planted in groups.

Polyanthus primrose (*P. ×polyantha*) is a hybrid primrose in a glorious array of flower colors. Individual flowers may be more than 1 inch across, some with large contrasting eyes, others a single color. They are arranged in umbels on stems typically 4 to 6 inches tall. Small, dark-green leaves are heavily veined.

For a constant succession of bloom, start with *P. rosea,* which flowers earliest in the season with rose pink blossoms. A month later, drumstick primrose, *P. denticulata,* produces lavender, white, blue, or pale purple flowers with small yellow eyes on 3-inch-diameter spherical heads. Next in succession are the candelabra primroses, which flower in whorls spaced along the stem. Japanese primrose, *P. japonica,*

is one type of candelabra primrose. Hybrids include 'Inverewe' with scarlet flowers, 'Miller's Crimson' with deep crimson blossoms, and 'Postford White' which is a pure and brilliant white. Tall-growing *P. pulverulenta* (tubular red flowers with dark eyes), *P. chungensis* (pale

Florinda primrose

orange flowers), *P. burmanica* (yellow-eye, rosy-purple or pink blooms), and *P. bulleyana* (yellow-orange flowers) are also candelabra primroses. A little later in the season, *P. sikkimensis* opens its umbels of fragrant white, yellow, or cream flowers. Last to go on display is the florinda primrose, *P. florindae,* which produces fragrant bright yellow blossoms.

Drumstick primrose

Pulmonaria saccharata
Lungwort

- **Hardiness Zones:** 3-8
- **Heat Zones:** 8–1
- **Light:** Half sun to shade
- **Size:** 15"H×15"W
- **Features:** Ornamental leaves and blue or pink flowers, early to midspring

Lungwort 'Bubble Gum'

An attractive plant in its own right, lungwort was valued by early herbalists as a cure for lung ailments because the leaves have a lunglike shape and bear white spots resembling those found on diseased lungs. Folklore aside, lungwort is a welcome sight in the shade garden.

Care: Plant lungwort in any well-drained soil that is either naturally rich or amended with organic matter. Plants tolerate either drought or heat, but not at the same time. They are prone to mildew. Plants self-sow and spread by stolons to form weed-smothering colonies.

Recommended plants and related species: 'Mrs. Moon' has pink buds that open to blue blooms and silver-spotted leaves. 'Pierre's Pure Pink' has pink-salmon blooms. 'E. B. Anderson' (*P. longifolia*) has blue flowers and silvery spotted leaves. Hybrids include 'Roy Davidson' (blue buds and flowers, silver-spotted foliage) and 'Sissinghurst White' (white blooms).

Rodgersia aesculifolia
Fingerleaf rodgersia

- **Hardiness Zones:** 5–6
- **Heat Zones:** 9–1
- **Light:** Half sun to shade
- **Size:** 2–4'H×3–6'W
- **Features:** Large leaves, ivory flowers, late spring

A foliage plant par excellence, fingerleaf rodgersia bears huge bronze-tinged leaves that resemble the fingers on a hand. Dense clusters of ivory flowers are held high above the foliage. The slow-growing plants act as a focal point among other coarse-texture species.

Care: Plant in well-amended soil that is rich in organic matter. Fingerleaf rodgersia does not tolerate heat or full sun; watch for wilting. Deadheading stimulates no additional bloom. However, deadheading improves the plant's appearance. Self-sowing is not a problem. Cut plants back in late fall or early spring. Division is rarely needed and plants are difficult to move.

Recommended plants and related species: Flowers of featherleaf rodgersia (*R. pinnata*) are more spread out along the flowering stalk, and the foliage looks less like a hand. The foliage of 'Superba' emerges bronze; flowers are pale pink. Leaves of 'Chocolate Wings' emerge brown, then turn green, bronze, red, and—in fall—brown.

Fingerleaf rodgersia

Rudbeckia fulgida
Black-eyed susan

- **Hardiness Zones:** 3–8
- **Heat Zones:** 9–2
- **Light:** Full to half sun
- **Size:** 2–5'H×2–3'W
- **Features:** Gold sunray daisies, mid- to late summer

Black-eyed susan 'Goldsturm'

The handsome foliage and brassy gold flowers of black-eyed susan are a sure sign of summer, and provides most perennial gardens with a sturdy, dependable plant.

Care: Plants tolerate a wide variety of soils, including ones that are wet and poorly drained. They also tolerate wind, coastal conditions, and heat. Divide every four to five years to maintain vigor, size, and quantity of bloom. Plants have running roots and are easy to move. Cut plants back in late fall or, if leaving seedheads through winter, in early spring.

Recommended plants and related species: 'Goldsturm' is a compact plant. 'Herbstsonne' grows 5 feet tall and has drooping sulfur-yellow blooms with green cones. Orange black-eyed susan (*R. fulgida* var. *fulgida*) begins blooming when 'Goldsturm' stops and continues into fall. Giant coneflower (*R. maxima*) has huge blue-green leaves and yellow flowers with prominent narrow cones. It grows 4 to 8 feet tall and 2 to 3 feet wide. The plant attracts birds and butterflies.

Salvia greggii
Autumn sage

- Hardiness zones: 7–11
- Heat zones: 9–4
- Light: Full sun
- Size: 30"H×30"W
- Features: Evergreen perennial; red, white, or lavender flowers over a long season in hot and dry climates

Autumn sage

Native to southwest Texas and northern Mexico, autumn sage is noted for its ability to produce masses of flowers through hot southwestern summers. Plants branch from a woody base and have leaves that are about 1 inch long. Flower stems rise 6 inches or so above leaves. Flower color is normally red, but cultivars with other colors are available. Flowers attract butterflies and hummingbirds.

Care: Follow a regular watering schedule during the first growing season to establish a deep, extensive root system. Reduce watering after plants are established. Prune old flowers to encourage reblooming.

Recommended plants and related species: 'Alba' is pure white; 'Big Pink' has an enlarged lower petal; 'Desert Blaze' is bright red and has variegated leaves; 'Furman's Red' has bright red flowers; and 'Purple Pastel' has lavender flowers.

Salvia nemorosa
Meadow sage

- Hardiness zones: 4–9
- Heat zones: 9–4
- Light: Full sun
- Size: 4–24"H×12–24"W
- Features: Violet or blue-violet flowers, late spring to early summer

Meadow sage is one of the showiest and longest-blooming of the cold-hardy salvias. Its flowers bloom in densely packed, narrow spikes. Plants grow in a clump at a moderate to fast rate.

Care: Plant meadow sage in any well-drained soil. Once established, plants tolerate heat and drought, but not high humidity. Deadhead as flowers age to prolong bloom. New flowering shoots develop near the stem's base. Some cultivars self-sow. Divide clumps every four to five years to rejuvenate; the forked taproot is increasingly resistant to division with time.

Recommended plants and related species: Dozens of hybrids are available, including 'Caradonna' (blue-violet, does not self-sow); 'Blue Queen' (blue flowers, self-sows), 'May Night' (indigo blue, does not self-sow); 'East Friesland' (deep purple, does not self-sow); and 'Marcus' (grows to only 4 inches tall and has blue flowers).

Meadow sage

Salvia verticillata
Lilac sage

- Hardiness zones: 5–8
- Heat zones: 9–1
- Light: Full sun
- Size: 18–24"H×18–24"W
- Features: Purple or white flowers over a long season

Lilac sage 'Purple Rain'

Native to the mountains of eastern Europe and the Middle East, lilac sage has naturalized in much of the northern and northeastern U.S. The olive green, fuzzy leaves are about 5 inches long. Near the base of the plant, they're typically divided into two or four leaves. Normally lavender blooms come in whorls containing 20 to 40, ½-inch-long flowers. Flowering starts in early summer and can last until fall.

Care: Like most sages, lilac sage prefers a sunny location that has well-drained soil. Remove faded flowers regularly to prolong bloom. Plants die back to the ground in fall but resprout from their roots.

Recommended plants and related species: Unnamed plants are seed-propagated and hence variable. 'Alba' has pure white flowers; 'Purple Rain' blooms are deep purple.

Saponaria ocymoides
Rock soapwort

- **Hardiness Zones: 3–7**
- **Heat Zones: 8–4**
- **Light: Full to half sun**
- **Size: 6–9"H×18"W**
- **Features: Rose pink flowers, mid- to late spring**

Rock soapwort

Rock soapwort is a great perennial for softening hardscapes. Let the bloom-covered trailing mat spill over walls or creep over a brick pathway. It is a good companion for sedum, coral bells, perennial fountain grass, blue oat grass, lavender, silver mound artemisia, rock cress, thrift, and bloody cranesbill.

Care: Plant rock soapwort in well-drained soil. Plants do not tolerate wet or poorly drained soil or hot, humid summers. Shear them after they bloom to promote density, make the plant neater, and reduce self-sowing. Self-sown volunteers are almost always available to save you the trouble of division. Divide rock soapwort in spring as desired. Plants have a running root. They are basically pest free.

Recommended plants and related species: 'Rubra Compacta' is red-violet and not as wide spreading. 'Max Frei' *(S. ×lempergii)* spreads less aggressively.

Scabiosa caucasica
Pincushion flower

- **Hardiness Zones: 3–7**
- **Heat Zones: 12–7**
- **Light: Full to half sun**
- **Size: 16–24"H×18"W**
- **Features: Blue-violet, pink, or white flowers, early to midsummer**

The blue-violet, pink, or creamy white flowers look like wide lace trim around a pincushion. Wiry flower stalks rise up to 30 inches above the mostly basal foliage. Plants grow at a moderate rate. Because flowers float far above their own insubstantial foliage, combine them with more substantial plants.

Care: Pincushion flower prefers sandy, well-drained soil. Plants tolerate wind and a wide pH range, but not high heat or humidity. Deadhead to prolong bloom, cutting first side branches with flower buds, then removing the entire flowering stem. The plant readily self-sows. Seedling flower color varies. Divide plants every three to four years to maintain good flowering and overall vigor.

Recommended plants and related species: 'Fama' has large, deep-blue blooms on 16-inch stems. 'Butterfly Blue' and 'Pink Mist', are long blooming, compact cultivars of *S. columbaria*.

Pincushion flower

Sedum spectabile
Showy sedum

- **Hardiness Zones: 3–9**
- **Heat Zones: 10–1**
- **Light: Full sun**
- **Size: 1–2'H×2'W**
- **Features: Broccoli-shape heads of pink, rose, or white flowers, late summer**

Showy sedum 'Meteor'

One of the most popular perennials for its foolproof nature and long-season effect, showy sedum is a clump-forming, fast-growing perennial.

Care: Plant in well-drained soil that is enriched with organic matter. Plants tolerate wind, heat, and high humidity, but not wet soil or poor drainage. Staking is not needed unless clumps are overcrowded or overfertilized. When temperatures reach 70°F in late spring, pinch stems to promote density. Divide offsets every four years to promote thick stems and heavy flowering. Leave spent blooms for winter interest. Cut off old stems in early spring.

Recommended plants and related species: 'Carmen' (dark mauve flowers); 'Iceberg' (white flowers); 'Meteor' (red flowers); 'Neon' (deep-pink flowers, an improved form of 'Brilliant'); and 'Stardust' (silvery pink flowers). Whorled stonecrop *(S. ternatum)* serves well as a shade-tolerant groundcover. It has white flowers and is hardy in Zones 4 to 8.

Sedum hybrids
Sedum

- **Hardiness Zones: 3–9**
- **Heat Zones: 9–1**
- **Light: Full sun**
- **Size: 1–2'H×2–3'W**
- **Features: Hardy plants with pink, rose, or white flowers, late summer into winter**

Sedum 'Vera Jameson'

Hybrid sedums have been among the most popular perennials in North American gardens over the last several years. Key reasons include their hardiness and success in varied situations and environments; their late-summer flowers that remain attractive even after fading to brown; and their compatibility with native grasses and other plants in contemporary naturalistic gardens.

All are colorful additions to a border of mixed perennials. They are not tall plants, so place them near the edge of a bed or where they can be seen. They also grow well in containers. Combine them with grasses, such as a dwarf fountain grass, or grasslike plants such as sedges. Matching hybrid sedums with flowering perennials such as 'Moonbeam' threadleaf coreopsis is also successful. The mature, dried seedheads of hybrid sedums are a favorite winter food for many birds.
Care: Plant in well-drained soil in a location that receives full sun.

Follow a regular watering schedule during the first growing season to establish a deep, extensive root system. Reduce watering after establishment. Feed with a general-purpose fertilizer before new growth begins in spring. In shade, or in warmer, southern regions, some cultivars become too tall and flop over. Cut them back in early summer to force more branching and more compact growth. Cut off faded flowers in spring when the new growth begins to show. Divide plants every three or four years to maintain a compact clump. Or, support plants with stakes or grow them adjacent to taller, stronger plants.
Recommended plants and related species: 'Autumn Joy' has been one of the most popular perennials for many years. 'Autumn Fire' is an improved form of 'Autumn Joy'. It has thick, strong stems that stay upright, and richer-color, longer-lasting blooms. 'Black Jack' has dark purple leaves and strong, upright growth. 'Frosty Morn' has green leaves with white borders and light pink flowers. 'Matrona' has stocky, burgundy-color stems and broad clusters of flowers that are maroon to pale pink. 'Vera Jameson' has leaves that are dusty plum-red, thick, and fleshy. The arching stems are purple; flowers are dusky rose. This is the most compact of all, growing 9 to 12 inches tall.

Sedum 'Matrona'

Sempervivum tectorum
Hen-and-chicks

- **Hardiness Zones: 4–10**
- **Heat Zones: Not rated**
- **Light: Sun to partial shade**
- **Size: 1–4"H×9"W**
- **Features: Evergreen, succulent leaves arranged in a symmetrical rosette**

Hen-and-chicks

Hen-and-chicks, also called houseleek, forms ground-hugging rosettes of tough, succulent leaves. The rosettes reach 6 inches in diameter. Clusters of red, purple, white, or yellow flowers rise on 15-inch stems.
Care: Hen-and-chicks is adaptable to most soils, even infertile ones, as long as the site is well drained. Plants tolerate drought. Water them occasionally in the heat of summer. Remove dead rosettes to make room for new growth. Propagate hen-and-chicks from seed or division.
Recommended plants and related species: 'Atropurpureum' has dark violet leaves. Leaves of 'Royanum' are yellow-green tipped with red. 'Sunset' has orange-red leaves. 'Triste' has reddish brown foliage. A naturally occurring variety of hen-and-chicks, *S. t. calcareum*, has broader leaves tipped with reddish brown. The leaves of houseleek *(S. arachnoideum)* are connected by cobweblike hairs at their tips; bright red flowers bloom in July.

Sidalcea malviflora
Checkerbloom

■ **Hardiness Zones:** 4–9
■ **Heat Zones:** 8–2
■ **Light:** Full to half sun
■ **Size:** 2–5'H×1–3'W
■ **Features:** Pink summer flowers

Checkerbloom

Reminiscent of hollyhock, checkerbloom has spikes of 2-inch single flowers in rose, pink, or white. It forms a mound of foliage that is topped by tall, straight, unbranched stems. **Care:** Plant in soil that is well-drained and rich in organic matter. Checkerbloom does not tolerate drought or a combination of heat and humidity. Deadhead for prolonged bloom and neater plants. Cut flowers off their stems just above a large lower leaf when the stem has more spent blooms than flower buds. Support, such as from adjacent plants or from a grow-through plant stake, is often needed to keep flower spikes upright. Cut plants back in late fall or early spring. Divide plants every three to four years to renew vigor; they have offsets. **Recommended plants and related species:** 'Party Girl' has light-pink flowers and grows to 30 inches. *S. oregana* 'Brilliant', with deep-rose flowers, also reaches 30 inches.

Sisyrinchium striatum
Argentine blue-eyed grass

■ **Hardiness Zones:** 3–10
■ **Heat Zones:** 8–3
■ **Light:** Full to half sun
■ **Size:** 1–2'H×1–2'W
■ **Features:** Yellow blooms, early summer

Argentine blue-eyed grass is a charming, flowerful perennial with grasslike, gray-green foliage. Its nearly 1-inch-diameter flowers appear in clusters on spikes. The plant's slowly expanding roots forms dense clumps over time. Use it as you would iris. **Care:** This beauty is tougher than it appears and withstands many garden conditions, including strong wind. Fertilize after flowering and then cut plants back to several inches above the ground to keep neat. Or leave faded flowers to mature and scatter seed, if desired. You can also increase plants by dividing clumps in early spring. **Recommended plants and related species:** Narrow-leaf blue-eyed grass *(S. angustifolium)* has delicate blue flowers with yellow centers, and pale green foliage. A clump former, it grows in bog gardens with other moisture lovers. *S. atlanticum* is similar to it.

Argentine blue-eyed grass

Solidago
Goldenrod

■ **Hardiness Zones:** 3–8
■ **Heat Zones:** 9–6
■ **Light:** Full sun
■ **Size:** 1–4'H×1–2'W
■ **Features:** Golden yellow flowers in later summer to fall

Goldenrod 'Golden Baby'

Wrongly reputed to cause hay fever, this plant is a lovely addition to a perennial garden. It combines wonderfully with daisy-type flowers, which bloom at the same time, and especially well with New England aster or white boltonia. Use goldenrod as a cut or dried flower. **Care:** Plant it in full sun in well-drained soil. Space plants 18 inches apart. Water in dry weather. Division of named cultivars is seldom necessary. Avoid wild goldenrods—they're usually running types, while cultivars are clumpers. **Recommended plants and related species:** 'Golden Baby' is 1½ to 2 feet with golden yellow blooms. 'Peter Pan' is bright yellow and stands 2 to 3 feet tall. 'Fireworks' *(S. rugosa)* has yellow flowers and red-tinged foliage. Seaside goldenrod *(S. sempervirens)* reaches 6 feet tall in Zones 3 to 11; true to its name, this plant thrives near the ocean in sandy soil, wind, and salt spray.

Spodiopogon sibiricus
Silver spike grass

- Hardiness Zones: 4–8
- Heat Zones: Not rated
- Light: Full sun to shade
- Size: 3–5'H×3'W
- Features: A bamboolike ornamental grass

Silver spike grass

Also known as frost grass, silver spike grass has bold, dark-green foliage that becomes brown with streaks and tinges of deep purplish red in autumn. Its shrublike form and long-lasting flowers make it perfect as a single specimen, planted in a group, or in masses. Silver spike grass looks wonderful with late-season perennials such as New England aster and sedum. Or, place it in front of evergreens that will highlight its airy flowers. Flowers and foliage look lovely in cut arrangements.

Care: Plant silver spike grass in well-drained soil in a location that receives either full sun or light shade. It will also grow in deeper shade but may require staking. Space plants 4 feet apart. Silver spike grass is not fussy about soil, but it prefers moist and well-drained sites. It performs best with regular watering or rainfall. Remove previous year's foliage in late winter.

Stachys byzantina
Lamb's-ears

- Hardiness Zones: 4–8
- Heat Zones: 9–1
- Light: Full to half sun
- Size: 4–6"H×12–18"W
- Features: Soft and fuzzy silvery leaves

This low-growing perennial is prized for its soft, silvery leaves. It also offers spikes of tiny lilac-pink flowers in early summer. Plants quickly grow into a medium-texture, gray mat that is useful for edging beds.

Care: Lamb's-ears grows best in well-drained, sandy soil. It does not tolerate high humidity, wet soil in winter, overly rich soil, or excess fertilizer. Clean up dead or rotted leaves in early spring. Fertilize at half the average perennial rate. The plant is typically grown for foliage rather than flowers. To maintain only the mat of leaves, remove the flowering stems as they appear, or grow a nonflowering cultivar such as 'Silver Carpet' or 'Big Ears'. Divide plants every three to four years to restrict their spread and renew the soil beneath the original planting.

Recommended plants and related species: Big betony (*S. grandiflora*) is a neat 1- to 2-foot mound of gray-green leaves with pink, white, or violet flowers on wiry 4- to 5-inch stems; Zones 3 to 8.

Lamb's-ears

Stipa gigantea
Giant feather grass

- Hardiness Zones: 6–10
- Heat Zones: Not rated
- Light: Full sun
- Size: 2–6'H×3'W
- Features: Fine-textured blades and golden flowers, early to midsummer

Giant feather grass

The golden flowers of giant feather grass, sometimes called needle grass, rise above clumps of 2-foot-tall foliage. In warm areas, plant with late-blooming perennials, such as New England aster, so they can fill the gap if the cool-season grass turns brown in heat. This grass is excellent used alone as a focal point, or in a mixed border. The flowers make fantastic bouquets.

Care: Plant giant feather grass in full sun in light, well-drained soil. Allow 3 feet between plants. Water regularly. It can stand hot, humid conditions and some drought; it does not survive waterlogged soil in winter.

Recommended plants and related species: Mexican feather grass (*S. tenuissima*) has a more fluid look, created in part by its silky flowers in June. Excellent in containers, it is heat-tolerant and hardy in Zones 7 to 10.

Stokesia laevis
Stokes' aster

- **Hardiness Zones:** 5–9
- **Heat Zones:** 1–9
- **Light:** Full to half sun
- **Size:** 1–4'H×1–2'W
- **Features:** Blue-violet, white, or violet flowers, mid- to late summer

Stoke's aster 'Blue Danube'

This Southern native is a fashionable, long-blooming perennial, attractive to butterflies. Short, fine petals make up its large, daisylike blooms. Plants are clump-forming and grow at a slow to moderate pace. They combine well with fine-textured companions, such as creeping thyme, artemisia, candytuft, and lavender.

Care: Plant stoke's aster in soil that is well-drained and rich in organic matter. The plant does not tolerate drought. Deadhead it to prolong bloom; flowers are on branched stems. After deadheading, only the basal foliage remains. Divide to renew plant vigor every four to five years; plants grow by offsets. Do not cut back for winter. Stoke's aster is basically pest-free.

Recommended plants and related species: 'Blue Danube' has blue flowers; 'Klaus Jelitto' has large, lavender flowers; 'Peachie's Pick' grows just 1 foot tall and has blue flowers; 'Omega Skyrocket' reaches 4 feet high and produces flowers on long but floppy stems.

Stylophorum diphyllum
Celandine poppy

- **Hardiness Zones:** 4–8
- **Heat Zones:** 8–4
- **Light:** Half to full shade
- **Size:** 18–24"H×12–18"W
- **Features:** Deep-yellow flowers, mid- to late spring

Celandine poppy brings gray and gold into the woodland garden. Its gray-green foliage is spangled with yellow flowers in spring. Plants are clump-forming and grow at a moderate to fast pace. Pair celandine poppy with yellow corydalis, gold-variegated hosta, purple-leaf coral bells, 'Brunette' Kamchatka bugbane, golden hakone grass, jacob's ladder, columbine, or bellflower.

Care: Plant in any soil that is rich in organic matter and shaded. Plants do not tolerate heat or full sun. Deadhead them if desired, by removing the branched flower cluster, although that seldom extends the bloom season. Plants self-sow; transplant seedlings to fill in the bed if needed. Division is not needed, nor do you need to cut plants back; foliage decomposes over winter. Don't confuse celandine poppy with greater celandine (*Chelidonium majus*), a weed that spreads aggressively by seed.

Celandine poppy

Tellima grandiflora
Fringe-cup

- **Hardiness Zones:** 5–10
- **Heat Zones:** Not rated
- **Light:** Half sun to shade
- **Size:** 8"H×21"W
- **Features:** Tiny green cups on long stalks, midspring

Fringe-cup

This dense-mounded evergreen perennial makes a fine edging for a shade garden and a gray-green point of contrast among forest greens, bronzes, and blue-greens. Its tiny fringed green cups bloom on wiry, naked stems. They age to pinkish green by midspring. Combine with blue-leaf hosta, columbine, meadow rue, bleeding heart, brunnera, purple-leaf coral bells, Kamchatka bugbane, barrenwort, or astilbe.

Care: Plant fringe-cup in well-drained soil that includes plenty of organic matter. Plants can tolerate drought and competition from tree roots, but they fail in soil that is wet, or where heat and humidity are high. Deadhead to keep plants neat, unless self-sowing is desired for naturalizing. Divide plants every four to five years to maintain vigor and renew the soil; they grow by offsets.

Recommended plants and related species: 'Purpurea' has more flower stalks and distinctly pink flowers.

Teucrium chamaedrys
Wall germander

- ▪ Hardiness Zones: 4–9
- ▪ Heat Zones: 12–4
- ▪ Light: Sun to partial shade
- ▪ Size: 6–12"H×12–24"W
- ▪ Features: Shiny green foliage and pink or purple flowers, summer to fall

Wall germander

Wall germander has evergreen leaves and bell-shape, tubular flowers that appear summer to fall. Growth is rapid by spreading underground root systems. Use it as a dwarf hedge, especially in or around knot gardens or in other formal settings.

Care: Plants grow best in any well-drained soil and full sun. They tolerate and even thrive in heat, and poor, rocky soil. They are also drought-tolerant and easy to maintain once established. Space plants 18 to 24 inches apart. Occasionally water in summer, but avoid overwatering. Shear straggly plants to encourage bushy, compact growth. The plants tolerate heavy pruning if done in early spring just after buds break. Propagate wall germander by seed or terminal cuttings.

Recommended plants and related species: 'Nanum' is a slightly more compact 10-inch-tall variety. 'Variegatum' has leaves variegated with creamy markings. 'Prostratum' is a ground-hugging, 6-inch-tall cultivar.

Thalictrum rochebrunianum 'Lavender Mist'
Lavender mist meadow rue

- ▪ Hardiness Zones: 4–7
- ▪ Heat Zones: Not rated
- ▪ Light: Full sun to shade
- ▪ Size: 3–5'H×2'W
- ▪ Features: Delicate, attractive leaves and pale lavender flowers in midsummer

Lavender mist meadow rue is a tall, airy, almost fernlike plant that is a good addition to woodland borders. Pale lavender flowers top the columnar, clump-forming plant in midsummer.

Care: Plant in soils that are moist and rich in organic matter. The more sun, the more water the plant needs. Lavender mist meadow rue does not tolerate heat and humidity or drought. Stake individual stems, especially where light is strongly one-directional. Divide after five to six years to renew vigor. The plant has running roots and is hard to move. Cut plants back in late fall.

Recommended plants and related species: Tall meadow rue (*T. dasycarpum*) grows to 7 feet, and is more drought-tolerant. Columbine meadow rue (*T. aquilegifolium*) grows 2 to 3 feet tall and looks like an upright baby's breath for the shade. Yellow meadow rue (*T. delavayi*) has lilac flowers with yellow stamens.

Lavender mist meadow rue

Thermopsis caroliniana
Southern lupine

- ▪ Hardiness Zones: 3–9
- ▪ Heat Zones: 8–1
- ▪ Light: Partial shade
- ▪ Size: 30–48"H×24"W
- ▪ Features: Bright yellow, lupinelike flowers in spring

Southern lupine

The bright, daffodil yellow flowers of southern lupine are a welcome sight in spring. Although native to the mountains of North Carolina, it performs beautifully throughout most of the Southeast, where lupines don't grow well because of the heat. Its blue-green leaves are divided into three leaflets, each about 3 inches long and covered in fine hairs underneath. The flowers come in 6- to 12-inch spikes and usually last for about a month. They make excellent cut flowers. Plant southern lupine in masses, in borders, meadows, or wildflower gardens.

Care: Grow in well-drained soil and in a location that receives full sun or partial shade. Plants are heat and drought tolerant. Cut back about a month after flowers fade, and propagate by either seed or division.

Recommended plants and related species: *T. chinensis* 'Sophie' grows only about 2 feet tall but has the same soft yellow, lupinelike flowers. It's hardy in Zones 5 to 8.

Thymus serpyllum
Creeping thyme

- **Hardiness Zones:** 4–8
- **Heat Zones:** 9–1
- **Light:** Full sun
- **Size:** 1–8"H×12–24"W
- **Features:** Evergreen foliage, white, pale pink, or violet flowers, late spring to early summer

Creeping thyme

From late spring to early summer, these fragrant evergreen mats are covered in tiny flowers. Plants spread by natural layering and can form large, dense colonies. They grow at a moderate to fast pace. Creeping thyme makes a fine edging with four-season interest. Or use it as an accent for larger, vase-shape perennials, such as butterfly weed, iris, and speedwell.

Care: Plant in well-drained, sandy soil. Plants tolerate half sun and shade from deciduous trees, as well as light foot traffic, drought, wind, and heat. Shear or mow plants after they bloom to promote density. Divide creeping thyme every three to four years to renew vigor. Cut out sections, fill the void with compost and sand, and allow perimeter plants to recolonize.

Recommended plants and related species: Many varieties have silver or gold variegation and distinctive scents, such as lemon or nutmeg.

Tiarella wherryi
Wherry's foam flower

- **Hardiness Zones:** 3–8
- **Heat Zones:** 8–4
- **Light:** Shade to half sun
- **Size:** 6–12"H×18"W
- **Features:** White to pink flowers, midspring

Wherry's foam flower is a lovely, small, clump-forming, woodland flower. It is aptly named after its foamy clusters of creamy white flower spires. Plants spread 12 inches or more by shallow under- or aboveground stolons, growing at a moderate to fast rate.

Care: Plant in any soil that is well-drained and rich in organic matter. Plants tolerate light foot traffic, but not drought. Divide plants every three to four years to reduce their spread. To maintain plant vigor, topdress with compost in late fall. Refrain from cutting plants back in fall.

Recommended plants and related species: Allegheny foam flower (*T. cordifolia*) spreads by stolons, making a great evergreen ground cover for shade gardens. Many cultivars of both foam flowers are available, with more being introduced every year. The hybrid cultivar 'Pink Bouquet' has light green leaves and pink-tinged flowers. Running varieties spread nicely and make good groundcovers. Look for 'Jeepers Creepers' or 'Running Tapestry'.

Wherry's foam flower 'Pink Bouquet'

Tradescantia
Spiderwort

- **Hardiness Zones:** 3–9
- **Heat Zones:** 12–1
- **Light:** Full sun to partial shade
- **Size:** 1–2'H×3'W
- **Features:** Purple, blue, pink, or white flowers, spring to fall

Spiderwort 'Sweet Kate'

This foolproof perennial produces abundant, showy, three-petal flowers in a variety of colors from spring to fall. It has grasslike leaves that look good spilling over the side of a woodland path. Plants do well in moist areas. Pair them with rose mallow, Japanese water iris, or columbine for an attractive contrast of textures.

Care: Spiderwort thrives in full sun to partial shade and moist, well-drained soil. After its first bloom in late spring, cut the plant back hard for fresh leaves, more flowers, and a tighter form. Keep it well watered in sunny locations.

Recommended plants and related species: 'Isis', rich blue flowers; 'Concord Grape', intense purple flowers and blue-green foliage; 'Little Doll' grows 10 inches high and doesn't flop; 'Purple Dome', dark purple flowers; 'Sweet Kate', yellow foliage and dark blue blooms; 'Osprey', white with a magenta-pink center; 'Hawaiian Punch', large magenta blooms; 'Caerulea Plena' (*T. virginiana*), double, dark blue flowers.

Tricyrtis hirta
Japanese toad lily

- **Hardiness Zones:** 4–9
- **Heat Zones:** 8–1
- **Light:** Shade to half sun
- **Size:** 2–3'H×2'W
- **Features:** Small but beautiful white flowers, late summer to fall

Japanese toad lily

Japanese toad lily is one of the most interesting plants for shade gardens, particularly in late summer or fall. That's when the purple-dotted, orchidlike flowers appear at each leaf axil. Plant it near a path or where you'll be able to appreciate the flowers closeup. The plant's arching stems add a textural note to the garden.
Care: Plant in rich, well-drained soil. Toad lily does not tolerate heat, drought, drying wind, or full sun. In cold areas, plant in half sun rather than deep shade to speed growth and ensure flowering before frost. Plants need neither deadheading nor staking, even in rich, moist soil. Stems arch outward to better display the flowers that are borne along the stems. No need to cut toad lilies back in fall or early spring. The stems and foliage decompose quickly over winter.
Recommended plants and related species: Formosa toad lily (*T. formosana*) blooms in mid- to late summer. It has spotted, dark violet flowers (Zones 5 to 9).

Trillium grandiflorum
Great white trillium

- **Hardiness Zones:** 4–7
- **Heat Zones:** 8–1
- **Light:** Shade
- **Size:** 1'H×1'W
- **Features:** North American woodland native produces white or pink flowers, spring

Great white trillum is perhaps the showiest and best-known spring wildflower of eastern woodlands. It's found as far north as northeastern Quebec, west to Minnesota, south to Missouri, and east to northern Georgia. The plants leaf out and bloom in early spring and die to the ground by mid- to late summer. Leaves are 2½ to 6 inches long and have wavy edges. The flowers are usually white or light pink and 2 to 3 inches wide.
Care: Plant in a shady woodland site in soil that is high in organic matter and that has a neutral to slightly acidic pH. Set rhizomes about 4 inches deep. Seed propagation is possible but takes much time, sometimes several years. Leave plants alone and they'll gradually increase in clump size.
Recommended plants and related species: 'Flore-pleno' is a dramatic double form. *T. grandiflorum roseum* is a dark pink form.

Great white trillium 'Flore-pleno'

Trollius hybrids
Globeflower

- **Hardiness Zones:** 4–7
- **Heat Zones:** Not rated
- **Light:** Half sun to shade
- **Size:** 2–3'H×3'W
- **Features:** Lemon yellow to orange globe-shape flowers, midspring

Globeflower and Siberian iris

Globeflower hybrids offer beautiful accents in spring. Blooms are layered globes of lemon yellow to orange, similar to large, double buttercups. They rise high above mounded, shiny foliage on strong, nearly leafless stems. Plants are clump formers and grow at a moderate rate. Plant globeflower with celandine poppy, Kamchatka bugbane, yellow corydalis, dropwort, golden hakone grass, and lungwort.
Care: Plant in rich, well-drained soil that includes plenty of organic matter. The plant tolerates a wide pH range as well as full sun if soil is constantly moist. It does not do well in drought or where the growing season is hot. Deadhead after bloom for neat appearance; the plant has branched flower stems. Plants rarely need division.
Recommended plants and related species: 'Earliest of All' flowers are pale orange-yellow. 'Lemon Queen' is a late bloomer with

Verbascum
Mullein

- **Hardiness Zones: 5–8**
- **Heat Zones: 7–2**
- **Light: Full sun**
- **Size: 18–48"H×18–24"W**
- **Features: Cream, yellow, pink, or purple flowers, early to midsummer**

Mullein 'Southern Charm'

A forgotten perennial just finding a spot in North American gardens, mullein has outstanding flower spikes that shoot up from a broad rosette of coarse leaves in early summer. Its coarse gray foliage complements blue foliage and contrasts with finer textures.
Care: Plant in well-drained, sandy soil. Plants resist wind, drought, and heat. They perform poorly in high humidity, in wet soil, or with poor drainage. Deadhead as seedpods begin to swell at the base of the flowering stalk. Or, because some mulleins are biennials, leave the last flowering stalk of the season to scatter seeds and propagate itself. Flower stalks normally do not require staking.
Recommended plants and related species: There are numerous new mullein cultivars, the best of which bloom two or three times in summer if deadheaded regularly. Look for 'Southern Charm' (salmon pink); 'Jackie' (cantaloupe orange flowers); or 'Plum Smokey' (purple flowers).

Verbena
Verbena

- **Hardiness Zones: 6–10**
- **Heat Zones: 12–1**
- **Light: Full sun**
- **Size: 1'H×3'W**
- **Features: Summer-long purple, pink, or red flowers**

Easy plants for all-season blooms, verbenas look great cascading over a rock wall, or in a rock garden. There are dozens of cultivars and species. Most form a glossy green, foot-tall mat of foliage that spreads out 3 feet or more. They are suitable for edging, growing as a groundcover, or potting in containers.
Care: Plant verbena in well-drained soil, and in full sun. Space plants 18 inches apart. You don't need to deadhead plants, but trim them back to keep them looking neat in early spring. Plants are prone to aphids, whiteflies, slugs, snails, and spider mites.
Recommended plants and related species: 'Homestead Purple' has large, dark velvety purple blossoms; 'Sissinghurst', bright pink blossoms with lacy foliage. Moss verbena *(V. tennuisecta)* has

Brazilian verbena

lavender flowers. Rose verbena *(V. canadensis)* has red or pink blooms in Zones 5–10. Brazilian verbena *(V. bonariensis)* bears tiny purple-blue flowers on 3- to 4-feet-tall, wiry stems from summer to fall. It's hardy in Zones 6 to 9 but reseeds heavily for a perennial effect in colder zones.

Verbena 'Homestead Purple'

Vernonia noveboracensis
New York ironweed

- **Hardiness Zones: 5–8**
- **Heat Zones: 9–1**
- **Light: Full to half sun**
- **Size: 3–7'H×1–2'W**
- **Features: Dark purple and red-violet flowers, mid- to late summer**

New York ironweed

For late-season color, few perennials match New York ironweed. It is a wonderful backdrop plant with large, flat-top flower clusters that is at home in informal beds and borders, as well as in a wildflower garden. Plants are upright, columnar, or vase-shape. New York ironweed's coarse, dark-green foliage complements ornamental grasses, thinleaf sunflower, purple bush clover, culver's root, and black-eyed susan, and its flowers attract butterflies.

Care: Plant in well-drained soil that is rich in organic matter. Stems can be pinched several times between spring and early summer to promote density and reduce height. Divide these long-lived plants after seven to eight years to maintain vigor and free flowering. They grow by offsets and are easy to move. Cut back plants in late fall or early spring.

Recommended plants and related species: There are many ironweed species that vary in height, color, and size of flowers and leaves.

Veronica longifolia
Long-leaf speedwell

- **Hardiness Zones: 4–8**
- **Heat Zones: 9–1**
- **Light: Full to half sun**
- **Size: 12–36"H×18"W**
- **Features: Blue flower spikes, midsummer**

Long-leaf speedwell is excellent in the middle of a border, in a rock garden, or clustered as specimen plants. Use long-leaf speedwell as a vertical accent for plants such as catmint and black-eyed susan.

Care: Plant in well-drained soil that is rich in organic matter. Long-leaf speedwell is wind-resistant, but does not tolerate drought, wet soil, or high humidity. Deadhead to prolong bloom. Divide plants every four to five years to maintain vigor and free flowering. Cut plants back in late fall or early spring. Leaf spot and mildew can be problems.

Recommended plants and related species: 'Blue Giant', with lavender-blue flowers, is 3 feet tall. 'Goodness Grows' has long-lasting blue flowers and grows 12 inches tall; 'Tickled Pink' is the same except for color. Alpine speedwell (*V. alpina*) is a 4- to 8-inch-tall spring-blooming miniature. Spike speedwell (*V. spicata*) has blue, pink, or white blooms. 'Royal Candles', a hybrid with dark blue blooms, reaches 18 to 24 inches.

Long-leaf speedwell 'Royal Candles'

Veronicastrum virginicum
Culver's root

- **Hardiness Zones: 4–8**
- **Heat Zones: 8–3**
- **Light: Half to full sun**
- **Size: 4–6'H×1–2'W**
- **Features: White to pale pink flower spires, midsummer**

Culver's root

Culver's root is a giant architectural perennial that is appropriate for the back of the garden. It grows in clumps at a moderate rate, producing flowers resembling sharp spikes. Use it to provide a vertical contrast to mounded plants, such as hardy hibiscus or mountain bluet. Its flowers also contrast nicely with black-eyed susan and yarrow.

Care: Plant culver's root in moist soil that is rich in organic matter. The plant grows well in hot climates. Deadhead to prolong bloom. Cut plants back in late fall or early spring. Plants are basically pest free.

Recommended plants and related species: 'Roseum' flowers have a notable pink flush, and flowers of 'Lavender Towers' are a beautiful soft lavender.

USDA Plant Hardiness Zone Map

This map of climate zones helps you select plants for your garden that will survive a typical winter in your region. The United States Department of Agriculture (USDA) developed the map, basing the zones on the lowest recorded temperatures across North America. Zone 1 has the coldest winters and Zone 11 has the warmest.

Plants are classified by the coldest temperature and zone they can endure. For example, plants hardy to Zone 6 survive where winter temperatures drop to –10°F. Those hardy to Zone 8 would die long before it's that cold. Perennials may grow in colder regions, but must be replaced each year. Plants rated for a range of hardiness zones can usually survive winter in the coldest region as well as tolerate the summer heat of the warmest one.

To find your hardiness zone, note the approximate location of your community on the map, then match the color marking your home area to the key.

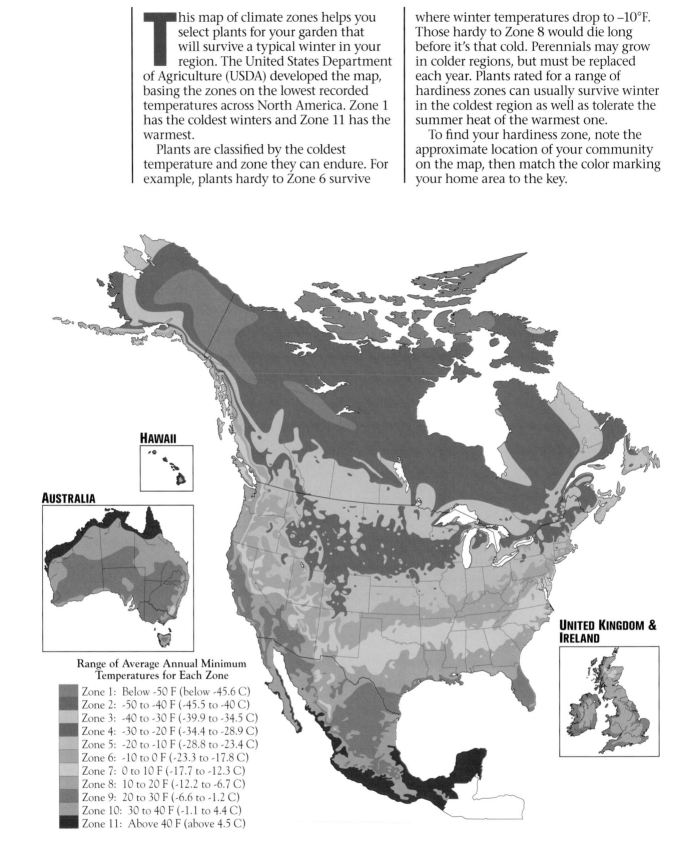

HAWAII

AUSTRALIA

UNITED KINGDOM & IRELAND

Range of Average Annual Minimum Temperatures for Each Zone

Zone 1: Below -50 F (below -45.6 C)
Zone 2: -50 to -40 F (-45.5 to -40 C)
Zone 3: -40 to -30 F (-39.9 to -34.5 C)
Zone 4: -30 to -20 F (-34.4 to -28.9 C)
Zone 5: -20 to -10 F (-28.8 to -23.4 C)
Zone 6: -10 to 0 F (-23.3 to -17.8 C)
Zone 7: 0 to 10 F (-17.7 to -12.3 C)
Zone 8: 10 to 20 F (-12.2 to -6.7 C)
Zone 9: 20 to 30 F (-6.6 to -1.2 C)
Zone 10: 30 to 40 F (-1.1 to 4.4 C)
Zone 11: Above 40 F (above 4.5 C)

AMERICAN HORTICULTURAL SOCIETY PLANT HEAT ZONE MAP

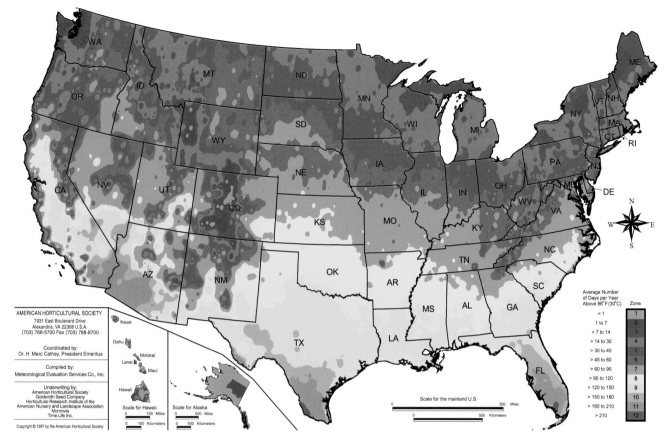

AMERICAN HORTICULTURAL SOCIETY
7931 East Boulevard Drive
Alexandria, VA 22308 U.S.A.
(703) 768-5700 Fax (703) 768-8700

Coordinated by:
Dr. H. Marc Cathey, President Emeritus

Compiled by:
Meteorological Evaluation Services Co., Inc.

Underwriting by:
American Horticultural Society
Goldsmith Seed Company
Horticultural Research Institute of the
American Nursery and Landscape Association
Monrovia
Time Life Inc.

Copyright © 1997 by the American Horticultural Society

Average Number of Days per Year Above 86°F (30°C)	Zone
< 1	1
1 to 7	2
> 7 to 14	3
> 14 to 30	4
> 30 to 45	5
> 45 to 60	6
> 60 to 90	7
> 90 to 120	8
> 120 to 150	9
> 150 to 180	10
> 180 to 210	11
> 210	12

Scale for Hawaii
0   100 Miles
0   100 Kilometers

Scale for Alaska
0   500 Miles
0   500 Kilometers

Scale for the mainland U.S.
0   500 Miles
0   500 Kilometers

METRIC CONVERSIONS

U.S. UNITS TO METRIC EQUIVALENTS			METRIC EQUIVALENTS TO U.S. UNITS		
To Convert From	Multiply by	To Get	To Convert From	Multiply by	To Get
Inches	25.4	Millimeters	Millimeters	0.0394	Inches
Inches	2.54	Centimeters	Centimeters	0.3937	Inches
Feet	30.48	Centimeters	Centimeters	0.0328	Feet
Feet	0.3048	Meters	Meters	3.2808	Feet
Yards	0.9144	Meters	Meters	1.0936	Yards
Square inches	6.4516	Square centimeters	Square centimeters	0.1550	Square inches
Square feet	0.0929	Square meters	Square meters	10.764	Square feet
Square yards	0.8361	Square meters	Square meters	1.1960	Square yards
Acres	0.4047	Hectares	Hectares	2.4711	Acres
Cubic inches	16.387	Cubic centimeters	Cubic centimeters	0.0610	Cubic inches
Cubic feet	0.0283	Cubic meters	Cubic meters	35.315	Cubic feet
Cubic feet	28.316	Liters	Liters	0.0353	Cubic feet
Cubic yards	0.7646	Cubic meters	Cubic meters	1.308	Cubic yards
Cubic yards	764.55	Liters	Liters	0.0013	Cubic yards

To convert from degrees Fahrenheit (F) to degrees Celsius (C), first subtract 32, then multiply by 5/9.

To convert from degrees Celsius to degrees Fahrenheit, multiply by 9/5, then add 32.

INDEX

Note: Page references in bold type refer to Plant Gallery entries. Page references in italic type refer to additional photos. Page references followed by asterisks refer to plant lists. Plants are listed by their common names.

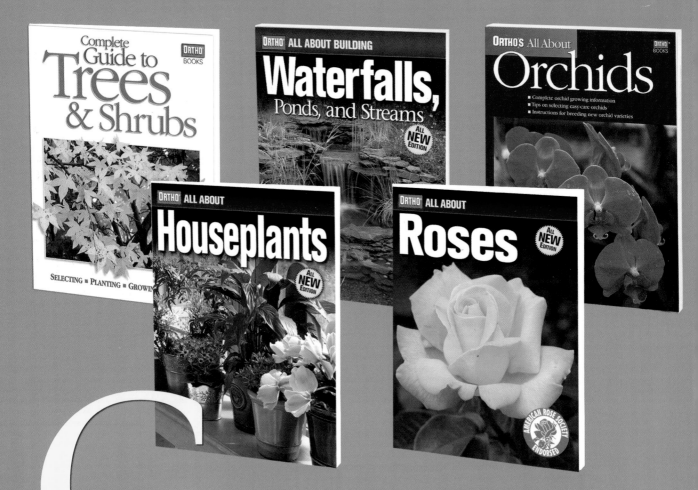